NEW Grammar Time 3

PEARSON
Longman

Sandy Jervis and Maria Carling

Pearson Education Limited
Edinburgh Gate
Harlow
Essex CM20 2JE
England
and Associated Companies throughout the world.

www.longman.com

© Pearson Education Limited 2008

The right of Sandy Jervis and Maria Carling to be identified as
author of this Work has been asserted by her in accordance
with the Copyright, Designs and Patents Act 1988.

*All rights reserved; no part of this publication may be reproduced,
stored in a retrieval system, or transmitted in any form or by any means,
electronic, mechanical, photocopying, recording, or otherwise without the
prior written permission of the Publishers.*

First Published in 2001
This edition 2008

Student Book ISBN: 978-1-4058-5272-2
Multi-Rom ISBN: 978-1-4058-5271-5
Pack ISBN: 978-1-4058-6699-6

Printed and bound in Romania by G. Canale & C. SRL.
Illustrations and cover by Mackerel Design
Designed and Project Managed by Starfish Design

Contents

1 *be*, subject pronouns

1 Complete the tables.

Statements		
Positive	I	am ('m)
	You / We / They	.... ('re)
	He / She / It	is ('..................)
Negative	I	am not
	You / We / They	.... (aren't)
	He / She / It	.... (isn't)

Questions		Short answers
....	I?	Yes, I .... No, I'm not.
Are	you? / we? / ....?	Yes, you / we / they are. No, you / we / they aren't.
Is	he? / she? / it?	Yes, he / she / it .... No, he / she / it isn't.

Wh- questions	
What / Who am	I?
Where / Who	you? / we? / they?
Where / Who is	..................? / ....? / ....?

2 Read the information.

be

- We can use a noun, an adjective or a phrase with a preposition after ***be***:
  I'm a student. *He's tall.*
  They're in the kitchen.
- In the negative, there are two short forms for ***is not*** and ***are not***:
  She isn't English. / She's not English.
  We aren't thirsty. / We're not thirsty.
- We usually use the short form of the verb when we speak.
  I'm not very hungry. *Lucy isn't here.*
- When we answer *yes* to a question, we can't use the short form of the verb.
  A: *Are these your glasses?*
  B: *Yes, they are.* ✔ ~~*Yes, they're.*~~

Subject pronouns

- We can use **subject pronouns** (*I*, *you*, *he*, *she*, *it*, *we*, *they*) instead of a name or noun:
  Peter's in my class. ***He****'s my friend.*
  The boys are at home. ***They****'re in the garden.*
- We use ***it*** for things and animals. But we often use ***he*** and ***she*** for pets, when we know the gender of an animal.
  This is Cosmo. ***He****'s my cat.*
  This is Bella. ***She****'s my cat.*

3 Complete with *am*, *is* or *are*.

1 Peter and Harry ..*are*.......... neighbours.
2 Beth .... a reporter for *TeenLink*.
3 Here's a copy of *TeenLink*. It .... the new school magazine.
4 Cosmo and Bella .... Harry's cats.
5 Look, there's Lucy. She .... Peter's sister.
6 Hi, I .... Kim. What's your name?
7 My friend and I .... in the school football team.
8 Hurry up! You .... late for school!

4 Complete with one word.

1 A: Hello. [1]*I*................'m Kate and this is my brother. His name [2]................ David. We [3]................ from London.
B: Hi. I' [4]................ Sarah.

2 A: What's this?
B: [5]................'s a present for Sam. It [6]................ his birthday today.

3 A: Where's Michael?
B: [7]................'s in his room. And Eva [8]................ in the living room.
A: Eva? No, she isn't. [9]................'s in the garden.

4 A: Look. Here are the photos from my birthday party.
B: Wow! [10]................'re great.
A: This is Anna. She [11]................ my best friend. And this is my brother, Matt. [12]................'re twins.

5 Complete. Use short forms.

1 A: Beth's eight. B: Beth isn't eight. She's .... twelve.
2 A: Harry's at school. B: .... at home.
3 A: Peter and Harry are cousins. B: .... friends.
4 A: London's in China. B: .... in England.
5 A: Giraffes are short. B: .... tall.
6 A: Italy is a big city. B: .... a country!
7 A: You're Tim's sister. B: .... his friend.
8 A: Anna's from Turkey. B: .... from Spain.

6 Write questions and short answers.

1 Peter / Lucy's cousin?
Is Peter Lucy's cousin? .... No, he isn't. ....

2 Cosmo and Bella / dogs?
....

3 Beth / a doctor?
....

4 Peter and Harry / neighbours?
....

5 Lucy / Harry's sister?
....

6 Harry / Peter's friend?
....

7 Peter and Lucy / twins?
....

8 *TeenLink* / the new school magazine?
....

7 Match and write the answers.

Geography Twelve Class 8c Ben London 1.5 metres

1 What's your name? ....
2 How old are you? ....
3 Where are you from? ....
4 What class are you in? ....
5 What's your favourite subject? ....
6 How tall are you? ....

8 **Write questions. Then write true answers.**

1 how old / you? How old are you? .... I'm ....
2 when / your birthday? ....
3 you / a student? ....
4 where / your school? ....
5 your classroom / big? ....
6 what / your teacher's name? ....
7 what / in your bag? ....
8 English / your favourite subject? ....

Writing practice

9 **Read and complete.**

TeenLink

Hi! I'm Harry! [1] (I/be/twelve) ....I'm twelve.... years old and [2] (I/be/the editor) .... of 'TeenLink,' our school magazine! [3] (I/be/in class 6C) .... and my teacher is Miss Green. [4] (My classroom/be/not/very big) ...., but it's nice.

My favourite subjects are English and History.

My best friend is Peter. We are in the same class and [5] (we/be/neighbours) ...., too!

What about you? What is your teacher's name? [6] (your classroom/be/big) ....? What are your favourite subjects? Who is your best friend?

Write to 'TeenLink' about you!

Harry Davis

10 **Write.**

Write to *TeenLink*. Use Exercise 9 as an example.

Write your name, age and class.
Write about: your teacher
your classroom
your favourite subjects
your best friend(s).

Dear 'TeenLink',

I'm .... and I'm ....

I'm in class .... My teacher ....

....

....

....

2 Demonstratives, *a / an / the*, plural nouns

Demonstratives, *a / an / the*

1 Complete the tables.

this / that, these / those	Singular	Plural
←	This is an umbrella.	……………… are sweets.
←	………………'s a rucksack.	Those are biscuits.

a / an, the
This is an apple. The apple is for Lucy. These are biscuits. …………… biscuits are for me.

2 Read the information.

this* / *that*, *these* / *those

- We use ***this*** and ***these*** to talk about someone or something that is near to us. We use ***this*** with singular nouns and ***these*** with plural nouns.
  This *is my friend, Harry.*
  These *are my cats, Cosmo and Bella.*
- We use ***that*** and ***those*** to talk about someone or something that is further away. We use ***that*** with singular nouns and ***those*** with plural nouns.
  That's *my brother over there.*
  Those *are his friends, Bob and Tim.*
- In short answers, we use subject pronouns (*it, they,* etc.), not *this* / *that* / *these* / *those*.
  A: *Is* ***that*** *your bag?*
  B: *Yes,* ***it*** *is.* ✔ ~~*Yes, that is.*~~
  A: *Are* ***those*** *your books?*
  B: *Yes,* ***they*** *are.* ✔ ~~*Yes, those are.*~~

a* / *an

- We use ***a*** **/** ***an*** with singular nouns to talk about one thing or person.
- We use ***a*** before words that begin with consonants (*b, c, d, f, g, h, j, k, l, m, n, p, q, r, s, t, v, w, x, y, z*) and ***an*** before words that begin with vowels (*a, e, i, o, u*):
  a *magazine* ***a*** *red umbrella*
  an *apple* ***an*** *expensive car*

***a* / *an*, *the* and plurals**

- We don't use ***a*** **/** ***an*** with plural nouns.
  a book ✔ ~~*a books*~~
- We can use ***the*** with singular and plural nouns.
  the *car* ✔ ***the*** *cars* ✔
- We usually use ***a*** **/** ***an*** when we talk about something for the first time, and ***the*** when we talk about it again. Compare:
  This is ***a*** *sandwich and that's* ***an*** *apple.*
  The *sandwich is for you and* ***the*** *apple is for me.*

3 Write.

	Singular	Plural		Singular	Plural
1	this boy	*these* boys	7	this apple	.... apples
2	that house	.... houses	8	.... plane	those planes
3	.... sweet	these sweets	9	that T-shirt	.... T-shirts
4	.... book	those books	10	this car	.... cars
5	that tree	.... trees	11	.... star	these stars
6	.... desk	these desks	12	.... umbrella	those umbrellas

4 Circle the correct answer.

1 [1] This / These are the photos from Sarah's birthday party. [2] This / These is my brother. [3] This / These is my friend, Pippa and [4] this / these is her cousin, Jack.

2 [5] This / These is my bedroom. [6] That / Those is my computer. And [7] that / these are my computer games. [8] This / These game is fantastic!

3 [9] This / These postcard is for you. [10] This / Those letters are for Mum. And [11] this / these magazine is for me!

4 [12] This / These biscuits are delicious! [13] That / Those sweets are nice, too. But [14] this / these chips aren't very good. And [15] that / those sandwiches are awful!

5 Write questions and answers.

1 '*Is this*......... your pen?'
'No, *it isn't*.........'

2 '.................... your sunglasses?'
'No, ...'

3 '.................... your cat?'
'Yes, ...'

4 '.................... your trainers?'
'Yes, ...'

5 '.................... your keys?'
'No, ...'

6 '.................... your phone?'
'Yes, ...'

6 Write *a, an, the* or – .

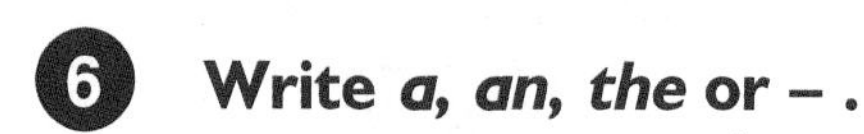

1 This is a T-shirt and that's a skirt. *The*...... T-shirt is black and *the*...... skirt is red.

2 This is .... orange and those are .... grapes. .... orange is for me and .... grapes are for you.

3 These are .... CDs and those are .... DVDs. .... CDs are cheap, but .... DVDs are expensive.

4 This is .... iguana and that's .... parrot. .... iguana is David's and .... parrot is Emma's.

5 This is .... desk and those are .... chairs. .... desk is for my room and .... chairs are for the living room.

7 Read and complete with *a, an, the* or – .

TeenLink

I've got two [1] .... cats, Cosmo and Bella. Here's [2] .... photo. [3] .... grey cat is Cosmo and [4] .... ginger cat is Bella. Cosmo is [5] .... boy and Bella is [6] .... girl. They sleep in [7] .... basket. Their favourite food is [8] .... fish fingers!
Harry

Plural nouns

8 **Complete the tables.**

Regular plurals

	Singular	Plural
-s	friend	friends
	apple	apple.....
-es	bus	buses
	beach	beach.....
-ies	strawberry	strawberries
	lady	lad.....
-ves	leaf	leaves
	knife	kni.....

Irregular plurals

Singular	Plural
man	men
woman	women
child	children
tooth	teeth
foot	feet
mouse	mice
person	people
sheep	sheep
fish	fish
deer	deer

▶ Look at the spelling rules on page 139.

9 **Complete the table. Write the plural of these words in the correct column.**

~~baby~~ boy city class computer day dress face family foot fox knife leaf lorry mouse pen person sheep shelf strawberry tomato watch wife wolf woman

-s	-es	-ies	-ves	Irregular
....	....	babies	....	....
....	....	....	....	....
....	....	....	....	....
....	....	....	....	....
....	....	....	....	....

10 **Form the plural.**

1 This photo is fantastic! *These photos are fantastic!*
2 That bag is heavy. ....
3 This story is very funny! ....
4 That woman is from London. ....
5 This dress is beautiful! ....
6 That boy is very tall. ....
7 This radio is expensive. ....
8 This knife is sharp. ....

11 **Complete with the plural form of the word in brackets.**

TeenLink

Animals around the world by Harry Davis

Koalas

[1] *Koalas*........ (koala) are from Australia. They've got big [2]................ (nose), yellow [3]................ (eye) and very strong [4]................ (foot). Their [5]................ (tail) are very small. Koalas eat [6]................ (leaf). They eat two [7]................ (kilo) every day. They love food!
They aren't dangerous, but they're afraid of [8]................ (person).

Tigers

[9]................ (tiger) are from Asia. They are very big [10]................ (cat) with strong [11]................ (leg) and sharp [12]................ (tooth)! They don't eat [13]................ (leaf), they eat meat. They eat a lot of [14]................ (deer). They also eat [15]................ (monkey) and [16]................ (fish). They are dangerous, but they're very beautiful.

12 Read, choose and write.

Mrs Hardy:	Here's your breakfast. [1] .... egg for Lucy and [2] .... sandwich for you, Peter.	1 a) A	b) An	c) –
		2 a) an	b) –	c) a
Peter:	[3] .... sandwich is for Lucy, Mum, and [4] .... egg is for me.	3 a) An	b) The	c) –
		4 a) –	b) an	c) the
Mrs Hardy:	Sorry! Here you are!			
Lucy:	Look, Mum! These are the right photos from [5] .... picnic.	5 a) this	b) the	c) a
Mrs Hardy:	They're good.			
Lucy:	[6] .... boys are from Peter's class.	6 a) These	b) This	c) –
Mrs Hardy:	Who's [7] .... boy with the dark hair?	7 a) a	b) an	c) the
Peter:	That's Ben. He's [8] .... new student in our school.	8 a) –	b) an	c) a

Writing practice

13 Complete with one word.

Hi! [1] *This* is my room. It isn't very big. [2] .... walls are green. I think it's [3] .... nice colour. There's a bed, a desk, a small table and [4] .... window. There isn't [5] .... TV, but there is a CD player.

This is my computer and [6] .... are my CDs. My desk isn't very tidy. Look! There are two [7] .... on it.

Look at those cars, over there, on the two [8] .... They are my favourite: [9] .... red car is a Ferrari and the green car is [10] .... Aston Martin. The [11] .... are from Australia. I like them very much.

14 Draw and write about your room.

Draw your room and write about it. Use Exercise 13 as an example.

Hi!
This is my room! ....
....
....
....
....

3 Possessive *'s*, *of*

1 **Complete the tables.**

Possessive *'s* (for people and animals)		
Singular	This is Harry's sandwich. That's Beth...... salad.	
Plural	**Nouns that end in *-s*** Here are the girls' milkshakes. Are those the boys...... bikes?	**Nouns that do not end in *-s*** What are the children's names? Look at those women...... clothes!

***of* (for things)**
What's the name of that street? What colour are the walls of the house? Look at the colour .... that car!

2 Read the information.

Possessive 's: singular

- We use **'s** or **'** to show that something belongs to a person or animal:
  Cosmo's basket *my parents' room*
- We add an apostrophe + -s ('s) after a name (*Peter's*) or a singular noun (*the cat's*):
  Peter's sister *the cat's tail*
- When a name ends in -s, we often just add an apostrophe, or the apostrophe + -s ('s):
  Charles' sister OR *Charles's sister*

Possessive 's: plural

- For plural nouns that end in -s, we just add an apostrophe (without the -s):
  my friends' house *the boys' names*
- If a plural noun does not end in -s, we add an apostrophe + -s (**'s**):
  the children's toys
- When we talk about something that belongs to two or more people, we add **'s** after the last name only:
  Fred and Sarah's house ✔
  ~~*Fred's and Sarah's house*~~

of

When we talk about something that does not belong to a person or animal, but is part of another thing, we do not use **'s**. We usually use a phrase with **of**. We say:
the walls of the house ✔
~~*the house's walls*~~
the top of the mountain ✔
~~*the mountain's top*~~ ✗

3 Complete.

1 Harry's computer is very good. (Harry)
2 Is .... birthday in July? (Helen)
3 Viv is my .... best friend. (sister)
4 .... violin is on her bed. (Lucy)
5 .... favourite food is fish fingers. (Cosmo)
6 That isn't .... ball! That's my ball! (David)
7 That .... mum is a teacher. (boy)
8 Where is .... bowl? (Bella)

4 Complete with *'s* or *'*.

1 Chris...... brother is a teacher.
2 I like Anne...... dress, but I don't like James...... T-shirt.
3 The girls...... shoes are under the bed.
4 My cousin...... CDs are on the desk.
5 Do you know Stella...... grandmother?
6 Giles...... house has got a lovely garden.
7 Jade...... bike is red.
8 My sisters...... room is very big.

5 Complete.

1 .... mum is a teacher. (Robert and Sophie)
2 The .... room is on the left. (children)
3 Who is your .... friend? (aunt)
4 My .... car is red. (parents)
5 I've got .... DVD. (Marie and Tess)
6 The .... bikes are over there. (women)
7 Where are .... bowls? (Cosmo and Bella)
8 We saw the .... father at the supermarket. (girls)

6 Put the apostrophe in the correct place.

1 My grandparents' house is in the country.
2 My friends names are Emma and Anna.
3 The childrens books are at school.
4 Those mens pictures are in the newspaper!
5 Phil and Davids rackets are in the wardrobe.
6 Charles eyes are green.
7 Those womens hats are exactly the same.
8 My parents bedroom is upstairs.

Look!
This is Amy's computer.
('s = possessive 's)
Amy's clever. ('s = is)

7 Write. Use full forms.

1 Bella's Harry's cat. Bella is Harry's cat.
2 That's Helen's mum. ....
3 Emma's bag's on the chair. ....
4 It's Jo's birthday today. ....
5 Mike's Sarah's cousin. ....
6 Sam's computer's fantastic! ....
7 Eric's father's a doctor. ....
8 My dog's name's Bono. ....

8 Write the answers.

1 A: Is this your bag? B: No, it's Tony's. (Tony)
2 A: Are these your books? B: No, ... (Mrs Cooper)
3 A: Is that your pencil? B: No, ... (Kevin)
4 A: Are these your glasses? B: No, ... (Mr Jones)
5 A: Is that your desk? B: No, ... (Ruth and Becky)
6 A: Are these your keys? B: No, ... (Diane)
7 A: Is this your notebook? B: No, ... (James)
8 A: Are these your sweets? B: No, ... (my brothers)

Look!
the top of the page ✔
~~the page's top~~

9 Complete with *of*.

1 Write your name at the top of the page, please. (top / the page)
2 Look, there's a cat on the .... (roof / that house)
3 The bus stop is at the .... (end / road)
4 I like the .... (colour / your dress)
5 Paris is the .... (capital / France)
6 The .... is very sad. (end / this story)
7 There's snow on the .... (top / the mountain)
8 There's a big garden at the .... (back / our house)

10 **Complete the questions. Use *'s* or *of*. Write true answers.**

1 What's the name of your street ? (name / your street)
2 What's .... ? (your teacher / name)
3 What colour are the .... ? (walls / your room)
4 What colour's .... ? (your dad / hair)
5 What's the .... ? (capital / France)
6 What's .... ? (your sister / favourite music)
7 Where's .... ? (the cat / food)
8 How old is .... ? (your friend / brother)

Writing practice

11 **Read and complete.**

TeenLink

***TeenLink* Best Friends Club.**
Tell us about your friends! Send a photo and a short note about your friends.

Lucy

Dear *TeenLink*,
My name is Lucy and I am eleven years old. This is a photo of my friends. We are in [1] dad's boat (dad / boat). The [2] .... (boat / name) is 'Lucy'! Sophie is my best friend. Ben is [3] .... (Sophie / brother).
[4] .... (Ben / favourite sport) is basketball. The [5] .... (dog / name) is Snowy. He's [6] .... (Ben and Sophie / dog). He's a great dog.
[7] .... (James / hobby) is skateboarding. He's very good!
[8] .... (Sandra / mum) is a singer! Sandra is a good singer, too.
Lucy Hardy

12 **Write.**

Write to *TeenLink* about your friends and/or family. Use Exercise 11 as an example. You can stick in a photo, if you like!

Write about their favourite:
sports
hobbies
pets

My name is .... and I am .... years old. This is a photo of my friends.
We are ....
....
....
....
....

4 *have got*, possessive adjectives and pronouns, *whose*

have got

There's an email from Harry's cousin, Adam from Australia. Adam Davis is 14 years old and he has got a twin brother, John.
1
2
Hi Harry!
Guess what! John and I have got new BMX bikes! They're birthday presents! I've got a green bike and John's got a red bike.
It's great because there's a BMX freestyle competition in our town next week.
Here's a photo of us on our bikes! Well, John isn't on his bike – he's on the ground!!
Cheers
Adam
PS: Have you got a BMX bike?

1 **Complete the tables.**

Statements		
Positive	I / You / We / They	have got ('ve got)
	He / She / It	has .... ('s got)
Negative	I / You / We / They	have .... got (haven't got)
	He / She / It	.... not got (hasn't got)

Questions			Short answers
Have	I / we / you / they	.... a bike?	Yes, I / you / we / they .... No, I / you / we / they haven't.
....	he / she / it	got a bike?	Yes, he / she / it has. No, he / she / it ....

2 Read the information.

have / has got

We use ***have / has got:***

- to say that something belongs to someone.
  I've got a new bike.
  He's got a camera.
- to describe someone or something.
  Peter's got dark hair.
- to talk about health problems.
  Claire's got a headache.
  I've got a cold.

3 Complete with *have got* or *has got*.

1 Mr and Mrs Davis *have got* a house in the country.
2 It .... a small garden and a small swimming pool.
3 They .... two children, Adam and John.
4 Adam and John are twins. They .... blond hair and green eyes.
5 They .... a dog, Bruno.
6 He .... long ears and a very long tail. He's very funny!

4 Write the full form of the verb.

1 She's my best friend. *She is my best friend.*
2 She's got blue eyes. *She has got blue eyes.*
3 Dave's Susan's brother. ....
4 Dave's got a new computer. ....
5 Becky's sister's got short hair. ....
6 Becky's twelve years old. ....
7 He's at home. ....
8 He's got a headache. ....

Look!

She's my cousin.
's = is

He's got dark hair.
's = has

Bill's parents are teachers.
('s = possessive *'s)*

5 Look and write. Then complete the table and write about you, too.

	laptop	camera	MP3 player	mobile phone
Samantha	✓	✓	✗	✗
Lee and Kim	✓	✗	✓	✗
....	....	....	....	....

1 Samantha / a laptop *Samantha's got a laptop.*
2 Lee and Kim / an MP3 player ....
3 Samantha / a mobile phone ....
4 Lee and Kim / a camera ....
5 Samantha / an MP3 player ....
6 Lee and Kim / a laptop ....
7 I / laptop ....
8 I / a camera ....

6 Write true answers to the questions.

1 Have you got a sister? Yes, I have. / No, I haven't.
2 Have you got a pet? ....
3 Have you got a bike? ....
4 Has your flat/house got a garden? ....
5 Has your best friend got dark hair? ....
6 Has your school got a swimming pool? ....
7 Have all your friends got mobile phones? ....
8 Have your grandparents got a car? ....

7 Memory Quiz: Look at the picture. Now cover it and write questions and answers.

1 Beth / black hair? Has Beth got black hair? No, she hasn't. She's got brown hair.
2 Harry / blond hair? ....
3 Lucy / brown hair? ....
4 Beth / a big nose? ....
5 Peter / a sister? ....
6 Harry / two cats? ....
7 Peter / blue jeans? ....
8 Lucy / a green shirt? ....

8 Complete with one word.

Hi!

My name's Christine and I'm from London. I'm thirteen years old. I [1] 've .... got long dark hair and brown eyes. I [2] ....n't got a brother or a sister, but I've got lots of friends. And I [3] .... got a parrot, too. His name's Chip. He's only one year old and he's [4] .... beautiful green eyes.

Please write and tell me about you. How old are you? [5] .... you got a brother or a sister? Have you [6] .... a pet?

Possessive adjectives and pronouns, *whose*

9 **Complete the tables.**

Subject pronouns	Possessive adjectives	Possessive pronouns
....	my	mine
you	your	....
he	his	his
she	her	hers
....	its	....
we	our	ours
you	....	yours
....	their	theirs

Whose		
Singular	Whose bag .... this?	It's hers.
Plural	Whose shoes are these?	They'............ mine.

10 Read the information.

Possessive adjectives and pronouns

- We use **possessive adjectives** (*my, your,* etc.) and **pronouns** (*mine, yours,* etc.) to show that something belongs to someone.
- We use *his* for a man and *her/hers* for a woman. We use *its* for things and animals. But we often use *his* or *her/hers* for a pet when we know the gender.
- We use a noun after possessive adjectives.
  This is my brother. His name is Rob.
  Is this your book?
- We don't use a noun after possessive pronouns.
  This is my book. ➜ It's mine.
  That's her bag. ➜ It's hers.
- Possessive pronouns usually come at the end of sentences.
  That ice cream's mine! It isn't yours!

Whose

- We use *whose* to ask who something belongs to.
  A: *Whose car is this?*
  B: *It's hers.*
  A: *Whose glasses are these?*
  B: *They're mine.*

11 Complete.

1 We're twins. ..Our.......... eyes are the same.
2 Look at that dog. .... ears are very funny!
3 That's Harry's best friend. .... name's Peter.
4 These are my cats. .... names are Cosmo and Bella.
5 The children are in the living room with .... friends.
6 We're from France. .... house is in Paris.
7 This is my brother. .... name's Brian.
8 Peter's got a sister. .... name's Lucy.
9 Please sit down and open .... books on page 28.
10 Hello. .... name's Kate and I'm thirteen years old.

12 Write.

1 This is my bag. It's mine.................
2 This isn't our garden. ....
3 That is your umbrella. ....
4 Those are his shoes. ....
5 That isn't their dog. ....
6 These are your books. ....
7 That is her hat. ....
8 Those aren't my keys. ....

13 Complete.

1 A: Whose......... glasses are............ these?
B: They're mine. (my glasses)
2 A: .... bag .... that?
B: It's .... (her bag)
3 A: .... house .... that?
B: It's .... (their house)
4 A: .... keys .... these?
B: They're ....! (your keys)
5 A: .... books .... these?
B: They're .... (his books)
6 A: .... jacket .... that?
B: It's .... (my jacket)
7 A: .... bikes .... those?
B: They're .... (our bikes)
8 A: .... pencil .... this?
B: It's .... (her pencil)

14 **Circle the correct answer.**

1 A: What's your / yours favourite subject?
B: Geography.
2 A: Is this book your / yours?
B: No, it's her / hers.
3 A: Whose is that red car over there?
B: It's our / ours.
4 A: Who are those girls?
B: That's Jo and that's her / hers sister.
5 A: Have you got our / ours tickets?
B: Yes, they're in my / mine bag.
6 A: That pen isn't your / yours. It's Tim's.
B: Oh, sorry!
7 A: Their / Theirs parents are doctors.
B: No, they aren't. They're teachers.
8 A: Are Ben and Michael here?
B: Yes. Those bikes are their / theirs.
9 A: Is that bag her / hers?
B: No, it's Anna's.
10 A: Do you like my / mine new T-shirt?
B: Yes, it's beautiful.

Writing practice

15 **Read, choose and write.**

STAR CORNER

You write about your favourite stars

Dear *TeenLink*,
[1] My.......... sister and I love comedy films.
[2]................. favourite film star is Ben Stiller.
We like him because [3]................. a very good actor and he's very good-looking, too! [4]................. short dark hair and [5]................. eyes are blue.
My sister and I [6]................. got all his films on DVD.
[7]................. favourite film is 'Night at the Museum' and [8]................. is 'Meet the Parents'. They're very funny.
Alicia (12)

	a)	b)	c)
1	a) Mine	b) My (circled)	c) We
2	a) We	b) Ours	c) Our
3	a) he's	b) his	c) he's got
4	a) He's got	b) His	c) Has
5	a) her	b) his	c) he's got
6	a) have	b) has	c) 's got
7	a) Mine	b) I'm	c) My
8	a) hers	b) her	c) she's

16 **Write to *TeenLink* about your favourite film star. Use Exercise 15 and the questions to help you. You can stick a photo in your book.**

1 *Who's your favourite film star?*
2 *Why do you like him/her?*
3 *What does he/she look like?*
4 *Have you got his/her films on DVD?*
5 *What's your favourite film?*

Dear 'TeenLink',
My favourite film star is ....
I like him/her because ....
....
....
....

5 *There is / There are*, prepositions of place

1 **Complete the tables.**

	Singular	Plural
Positive	There is ('s)	There are
Negative	There is not (isn't)	There .... not (aren't)
Question	Is there?	.... there?
Short answers	Yes, there is. No, there	Yes, there .... No, there aren't.

Prepositions of place		
in	opposite	behind
in front of	under	near
next to	on	between

2 Read the information.

There is / There are

- We use ***there is*** and ***there are*** to say that something or someone exists.
  There's a monkey near the swing.
  There are four cinemas in this town.
- In short answers, we use ***there***, not ***it*** or ***they***.
  A: *Is there a cinema in Rose Street?*
  B: *Yes, there is.* ✔ ~~*Yes, it is.*~~
  A: *Are there four cinemas in this town?*
  B: *No, there aren't.* ✔ ~~*No, they aren't.*~~

Expressions with preposition + noun

at school, at home, at work
My brother is at school. My mum's at work.
at the zoo, at the cinema
Peter is at the zoo.
My friends are at the cinema.
on the left/right
The supermarket's on the left.
in bed, in hospital
Lucy's in bed.
My grandmother is in hospital.

3 Look, read and complete.

Beth's desk

Lucy's desk

1 There's ...... a fairy cake on Lucy's ...... desk.
There's ...... a sandwich on Beth's ...... desk.
2 There are ...... two keys on Beth's ...... desk.
.... three CDs on .... desk.
3 .... a laptop on .... desk.
.... an i-pod on .... desk.
4 .... two magazines on .... desk.
.... four photos on .... desk.
5 .... a lamp on .... desk.
.... a pen on .... desk.

4 **Complete with *Is there* or *Are there*. Then answer the questions. Don't look at Exercise 3. How much can you remember?**

1 Is there .... an i-pod on Beth's desk? No, there isn't. ....
2 .... four photos on Beth's desk? ....
3 .... two keys on Lucy's desk? ....
4 .... three CDs on Lucy's desk? ....
5 .... a laptop on Beth's desk? ....
6 .... a lamp on Lucy's desk? ....
7 .... a fairy cake on Beth's desk? ....
8 .... two magazines on Lucy's desk? ....

5 **Look, choose and complete.**

next to   between   behind   opposite   ~~under~~   on

1 Where's Peter's .... T-shirt?
It's under .... the bed.
2 .... his shoes?
.... the bed.
3 .... his picture?
.... the door.
4 .... his football?
.... the toothbrush and the cap.
5 .... his guitars?
.... the chair.
6 .... the chairs?
.... the door.

6 **Read, choose and complete.**

at   in   on   to

Aunt Agatha: Hello, Lucy. Why are you [1] at .... home? Why aren't you [2] .... school?
Lucy: Because it's Saturday! And I'm [3] .... bed because I'm ill.
Aunt Agatha: Oh dear! Are Cosmo and Bella with you?
Lucy: Yes, they're here, next [4] .... me. Cosmo is [5] .... my left and Bella is [6] .... my right.
Aunt Agatha: Where's Peter? Is he at home?
Lucy: No, he isn't. He's [7] .... the sports centre with Beth. And Harry is [8] .... the cinema.
Aunt Agatha: Where are Mum and Dad?
Lucy: Mum's at the supermarket and Dad's [9] .... work. I'm so lonely!

Writing practice

7 Look, choose and write.

TeenLink

Dear *TeenLink*,
I live in a small town [1] (near) / in front of the sea.
My house is [2] in / next Petunia Street. It is [3] between / near a nice park.
In the centre of the town [4] there's / there are restaurants and shops.
[5] There's / Is there a big supermarket and there's also a cinema. There's a swimming pool [6] in / opposite the supermarket and a café [7] next / on to the cinema.
Here's a map!
Fred, 10

8 Write.

Write to *TeenLink* about your town/village. You can stick a photo in your book or draw a picture of your town/village. Answer the questions. Use Exercise 7 as an example.

1 Is your town/village big or small?
2 What street is your house in?
3 Is your house near a park / your school / the shops?
4 Are there shops / restaurants / cafés in your town/village?
5 Is there a supermarket? Is there a swimming pool / sports centre? Where are they?
6 Is there a zoo near your town?

Dear '*TeenLink*',
I live in ....
My house is ....
....
....
....
....

Use your English (Units 1–5)

1 Listen and tick (✓) the correct answer.

1 Where's Sarah's bag?

a  ☐

b  ☐

c 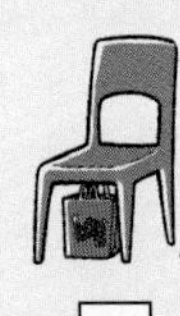 ☐

2 Where's the supermarket?

a  ☐

b  ☐

c  ☐

3 Which photo is from the birthday party?

a 

☐

b  ☐

c 

☐

4 Where's the cinema?

a 

☐

b 

☐

c 

☐

5 Where's the umbrella?

a  ☐

b 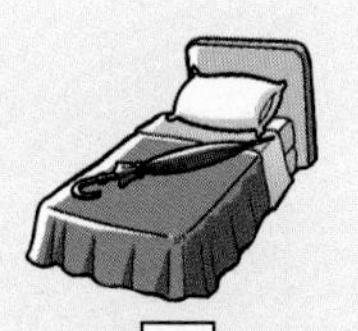 ☐

c 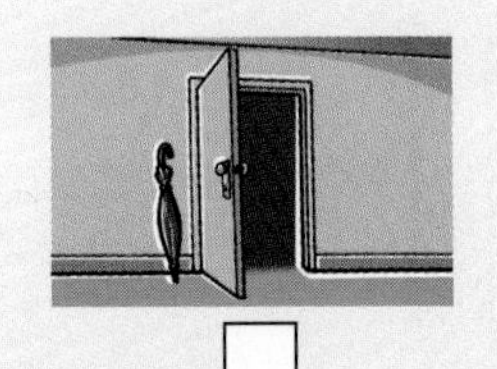 ☐

2 Circle the correct answer. Then choose a dialogue and act it out.

1 A: Is [1] that / those Ken's bike?
B: No, it isn't. Ken [2] has not / hasn't got a bike.
A: [3] Whose / Who is it, then?
B: It's [4] my / mine!

2 A: Are [5] this / these flowers for Mary?
B: Yes. It's [6] her / hers birthday today.
A: Oh no! I [7] have not / haven't got a present for her.
B: Don't worry. We can buy one now.

3 A: [8] Is / Are there a sports centre near your house?
B: [9] Yes, it / there is. And there's [10] a / the swimming pool, too – Rainbow Pool.
A: Rainbow Pool? That's next to my uncle's shop!

3 Choose and write the correct answer.

TeenLink

Reader's Corner

This week: Meet Jessica and Kevin

Hi!
[1] .... name's Kevin and I'm from London. I'm thirteen years old. I've got two brothers and [2] .... sister. My sister's name is Becky and my [3] .... names are Eric and Dave. Becky [4] .... seventeen. Eric and Dave are thirteen. [5] .... twins.
I love football and music.

Dear *TeenLink*,
I'm Jessica. I'm from Keymer. It's a small village [6] .... Brighton. There aren't many [7] .... here – it's very quiet. But [8] .... lots of friends [9] .... school. I love your magazine. [10] .... fantastic!
Well done!

	A	B	C
1	I	My	Mine
2	a	an	the
3	brothers	brother's	brothers'
4	is	has	has got
5	They	They're	Their
6	next	between	near
7	person	people	peoples
8	I've	I got	I've got
9	in	at	on
10	He's	It's	They're

4 Answer the questions about you. Write full sentences.

1 How old are you?
I'm .... years old.

2 Where are you from?
....

3 Have you got a brother or a sister?
....

4 What's your favourite subject at school?
....
....

5 What's your best friend's name?
....

5 Now write about a friend. Use the questions from Exercise 4.

1 .... is .... years old.
2 He/She ....
3 ....
4 ....
5 ....

Now you can ...

- ✔ Talk about yourself:
  My name's Katy. I'm from Cambridge.
- ✔ Describe people, things and places:
  Jo's got black hair.
  My bag is green.
  There are two cinemas in our town.
- ✔ Talk about possession:
  Sarah's bike is blue.
  My dad's got a red car.
- ✔ Say where things are:
  The dictionary's on your desk.
- ✔ Identify people and things:
  That's Lee.
  The blue notebook's mine.

6 Imperatives, object pronouns

1 **Complete the tables.**

Imperatives			
Positive	Stop.	Leave me alone.	Pull.
Negative	Do not (Don't) stop.	Do not (..................) leave me alone.	.... (Don't) pull.

Let's	
Let's	go. play football. make a cake. watch TV.

Subject pronouns	I	you	he	she	....	we	you	....
Object pronouns	....	you	him	her	it	us	....	them

2 Read the information.

Imperatives

We use **imperatives**

- to tell people what to do:
  Please close the door.
- to give instructions:
  Put the eggs in a bowl.
- to give advice:
  Be careful.

Let's

We use ***let's*** + the infinitive without *to* to make suggestions.

Let's play football. *Let's make a cake.*

Object pronouns

Object pronouns come after a verb. We use them instead of a noun or name.

They can't see Lucy. ➜ *They can't see her.*

Look at this photo. ➜ *Look at it.*

She can help Tom and Dave. ➜ *She can help them.*

3 Complete the instructions. Use the verbs in the box.

listen open tidy help look come

1 .... your room, please.
2 .... me, please!
3 .... here, please.
4 .... to your teacher.
5 .... your books on page 27.
6 .... at that boy.

4 Complete the sentences.

1 Please open the window. Don't open the door.
2 Wear the blue dress. .... the black dress.
3 Sit on the chair! .... on the table!
4 Buy the green jacket. .... the brown jacket.
5 Play in the garden. .... in the living room.
6 Call Emma. .... Sarah.

5 Complete the signs. Use full forms.

1 Do not walk on the grass. (not walk)

2 .... in cold water. (wash)

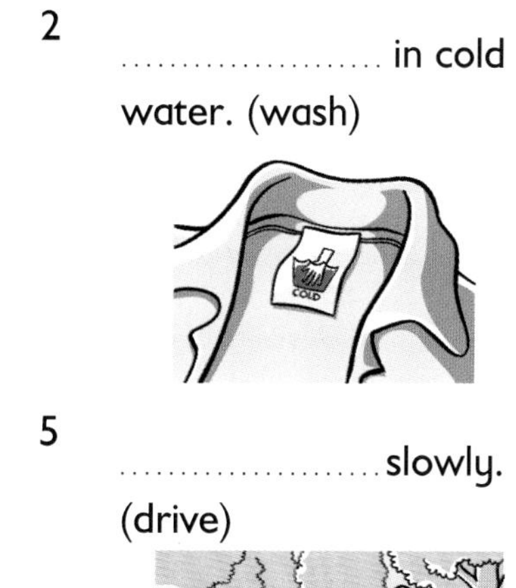

3 Please .... animals. (not feed)

4 .... photos. (not take)

5 .... slowly. (drive)

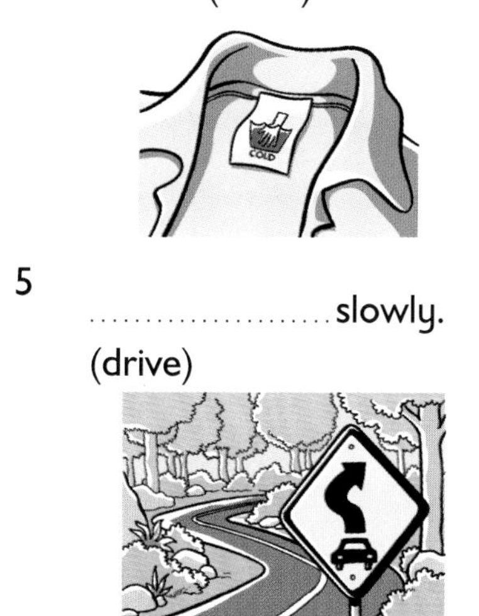

6 .... 856782. (call)

6 Complete the sentences. Use *don't* or *let's*.

1 It's really hot today. ....Let's.... go to the beach.
2 You can go to the cinema, but .... be late.
3 I'm tired. .... go home.
4 You must be quiet in here. .... shout!
5 .... go near that tiger! It's dangerous!
6 I can't find the museum. .... look at the map.
7 I'm hungry. .... make some sandwiches.
8 This isn't funny! .... laugh!

7 Circle the correct answer.

1 Can I / me use your computer?
2 We're busy. We / Us can't come with you.
3 I can't find my keys. Where are they / them?
4 Don't go. Stay with we / us.
5 Go away! Leave I / me alone!
6 Kate isn't here. She's / Her's in the garden.
7 Where are Cosmo and Suzie? I can't see they / them.
8 Emma's over there. Let's help she / her.

8 Complete the sentences. Use object pronouns.

1 Hey! Those are my CDs! Don't touch .... !
2 Look, there's Peter! Let's go and talk to ....
3 Where are you? I can't see ....
4 We can't carry this box. Please help ....
5 They're so funny! Look at .... !
6 I'm here. Look at ....

9 Read, choose and complete.

go Look us Don't be take Let's Don't touch it her

Peter: I'm hungry. [1] .... Lucy! There's a chocolate cake in the fridge!
Lucy: [2] .... it, Peter. It isn't for [3] ....
Peter: Yes, it is. It's in our fridge, isn't it?
Lucy: Leave [4] .... alone!
Peter: Come on, Lucy! [5] .... mean. [6] .... have a tiny slice.

Four slices of cake later ...

Mum: Hi, kids! Are you ready for Aunt Agatha's birthday party?

Lucy: Yes, Mum.

Mum: Peter, please [7] .... to the kitchen and [8] .... Aunt Agatha's birthday cake out of the fridge.

Peter: Aunt Agatha's birthday cake?

Mum: That's right, Peter. I always make [9] .... a cake for her birthday.

Lucy: Oh, no! Peter!

Peter: Run, Lucy! Run!

Writing practice

10 **Put the pictures in the right order.**

a Pour into a glass. ☐

b Put the fruit into a blender. ☐

c Slice the fruit. ☐

d Add ice. ☐

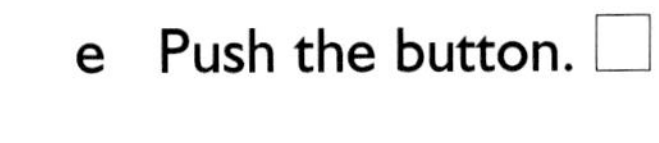

e Push the button. ☐

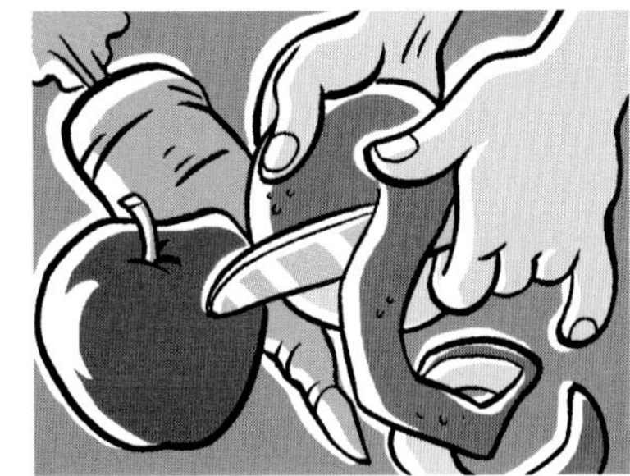

f Peel the fruit. ☐

11 **Write your recipe.**

Let's make a fruit cocktail!

Take an apple, a carrot and an ....

.... the fruit and then .... it.

.... the fruit into a ....

.... the button.

.... the fruit juice ....

Enjoy!

Present simple, time expressions

1 **Complete the tables.**

Statements		
Positive	I / You / We / They	play.
	He / She / It	plays.
Negative	I / You / We / They	.... not (don't) play.
	He / She / It	does not (doesn't) play.

Questions		
Do	I / we / you / they	....
Does	he / she / it	play?

Short answers
Yes, I / you / we / they do. No, I / you / we / they ....
Yes, he / she / it .... No, he / she / it doesn't.

Wh- questions			
What Where	do does	I / we / you / they he / she / it	play?

▶ Look at the spelling rules on page 140.

2 Read the information.

Use

- We use the **present simple** to talk about:
  habits, things that we do regularly:
  I go to school every day.
  facts, things that are always or usually true:
  My parents work in a bank.
  The Earth goes round the sun.

Form

- In positive sentences, we add -s or -es to the main verb in the third person singular (*he/she/it*).
  *I play the violin. She play**s** the violin.*
- In negative sentences and questions, we do NOT add -s or -es to the main verb for *he/she/it*.
  *He like**s** pizza. He doesn't like pizza. Does he like pizza?*

Time expressions

- We often use these time expressions with the present simple to say when something happens:
  ***in** January, **in** the winter, **in** the morning /afternoon/evening*
  ***on** Mondays, **on** Monday morning, **on** my birthday, **on** the 4th of August*
  ***at** seven o'clock, **at** midnight, **at** the week-end, **at** night, **at** Christmas*
- We also use these phrases to say how often something happens:
  every day/week/month/year
  once/twice/three times a week.
- They come at the beginning or end of the sentence.
  ***Every day** she meets her friends the park.*
  *Jon visits his aunt **every week**.*
  *We wash our car **once a week**.*
- We say:
  ***in** the morning* BUT ***on** Monday morning*
  ***at** Christmas* BUT ***on** Christmas day*
  ***on** Mondays* BUT ***every** Monday*

3 Write the third person singular of the verbs in the correct column.

~~answer~~ carry close cry fix fly go like start stay teach tidy wash watch worry

-s	-es	-ies
answers	....	....
....	....	....
....	....	....
....	....	....
....	....	....

Look!

vowel + *-y*: add *-s*:
play ➜ *plays*
consonant + *-y*: change *-y* to *-ies*:
study ➜ *studies*

4 Complete with the present simple.

1 Lucy *watches* her favourite cartoon at five o'clock every day. (watch)
2 Harry .... Lucy's music. (like)
3 The swimming pool .... at six o'clock. (close)
4 We .... my grandparents on Sundays. (visit)
5 Elephants .... leaves and grass. (eat)
6 My pen friend .... in Japan. (live)
7 I .... my room every morning. (tidy)
8 Our lessons .... at eight. (start)
9 Mr Allan .... Geography. (teach)
10 These birds .... north in the spring. (fly)

Look!
I get up at seven o'clock.
*Peter get**s** up at eight o'clock.*
I watch TV.
*She watch**es** TV.*

5 Read and complete.

Harry: Cosmo [1] *gets up* (get up) very late in the morning and he [2]................ (drink) his milk. Then he takes a nap. At lunchtime, he [3]................ (have) lunch and then he takes a nap.
In the afternoon, he [4]................ (play) with Bella, he [5]................ (watch) TV and then he takes a nap!
In the evening, he [6]................ (eat) his dinner and then …

Peter: … and then he takes a nap?

Harry: No, he doesn't. He [7]................ (go out) with his friends! He [8]................ (stay) out all night!

Cosmo looks tired!
Well, he's a very busy cat!
COSMO

6 Complete.

1 A: Lucy plays the piano.
B: She *doesn't play* .... the piano. She *plays* .... the violin.
2 A: Wayne and Sheila live in Cambridge.
B: They .... in Cambridge. They .... in London.
3 A: Harry writes books.
B: He .... books. He .... articles for *TeenLink*.
4 A: We have lunch at two o'clock.
B: You .... lunch at two. You .... lunch at one.
5 A: Pandas eat fish.
B: They .... fish. They .... bamboo leaves.
6 A: You drink a lot of tea!
B: I .... a lot of tea. But I .... a lot of milk.
7 A: My brother and I like football.
B: You .... football. You .... basketball.
8 A: You study French at school.
B: I .... French at school. I .... Spanish.

Look!
She doesn't play the piano. ✔
~~She doesn't plays the piano.~~

7 Look at the table. Complete the questions and write short answers.

	live in England	drink milk every day	play basketball on Saturdays	get up early on Sunday mornings
Peter	✔	✗	✔	✗
Lucy	✔	✔	✗	✗
Cosmo and Bella	✔	✔	✗	✗
Harry	✔	✔	✔	✗

1 *Does* Peter *live* in England? *Yes, he does.*
2 .... Cosmo and Bella .... early on Sunday mornings? ....
3 .... Harry .... milk every day? ....
4 .... Lucy .... basketball on Saturdays? ....
5 .... Cosmo and Bella .... milk every day? ....
6 .... Peter .... early on Sunday mornings? ....
7 .... Peter and Harry .... basketball on Saturdays? ....
8 .... Lucy .... in England? ....

8 Write questions. Then write true answers.

1 you / walk to school / every day?
Do you walk to school every day? *Yes, I do. / No, I don't.*
2 your lessons / start / at eight o'clock?
....
3 you / do your homework / every evening?
....
4 you and your best friend / go / to the same school?
....
5 you / watch / TV after school?
....
6 your best friend / visit / you at weekends?
....
7 you / play sport / every day?
....
8 your mum / get up early / at weekends?
....

9 Complete.

1 A: How often *do you go* to the cinema? (you / go) B: Once a week.
2 A: Where ....? (they / live) B: In Brighton.
3 A: What time .... to bed? (you / go) B: At ten o'clock.
4 A: How often .... tennis? (Sam / play) B: Every day.
5 A: What .... after school? (you / do) B: We play basketball.
6 A: How .... to school? (Zoe / go) B: By bus.
7 A: What .... for breakfast? (you / want) B: Milk and cornflakes.
8 A: Where .... work? (your sister / work) B: In a bookshop.

10 Match

1 How much flour do we need for the bread?
2 Do you live near here?
3 What sport does your sister like?
4 What time do you get up?
5 Does your father drive to work?
6 When is your birthday?
7 Do the children go to the park at weekends?
8 Does she live near you?

a Yes, they do.
b 500 grams.
c At half past six.
d Yes, I do.
e No, she doesn't.
f She likes tennis.
g In May.
h Yes, he does.

11 Choose and write. Are the sentences true for you? Put a tick (✔) or cross (✗) in the box.

at (x2) every (x2) in (x2) on (x3) twice

1 I stay at home ...at... weekends. ☐
2 I go to the park .... Saturdays. ☐
3 I get up .... seven o'clock .... Mondays. ☐
4 We have an English lesson .... a week. ☐
5 I watch TV .... the evening. ☐
6 We have a Maths test .... week. ☐
7 I see my best friend .... day. ☐
8 I go on holiday .... July. ☐
9 School starts .... the 3rd of September. ☐

Look!
What time do you get up in the morning? ✔
~~What time you get up in the morning?~~

12 Write the questions in the questionnaire. Then ask a partner and write the answers.

1 what time / you / get up / in the morning?
2 when / you / do / your homework?
3 what / you / do / in your free time?
4 how often / you / go / to the sports centre?
5 you / play / computer games?
6 you / listen / to classical music?
7 what time / you / go / to bed?
8 when / your family / go on holiday?

TeenLink

***TeenLink* Questionnaire**

YOUR PARTNER'S NAME: ....

1 *What time do you get up in the morning* ? ....
2 .... ? ....
3 .... ? ....
4 .... ? ....
5 .... ? ....
6 .... ? ....
7 .... ? ....
8 .... ? ....

Writing Practice

13 Read and complete.

Lucy has a Japanese pen pal, Izumi. She sends her an email every week.

Hi Izumi,
The school holidays are near! I love them! I [1] *get up* (get up) late in the morning. I [2] .... (not go) to school and I [3] .... (not have) homework!
My friend Sophie [4] .... (come) to my house every day and we [5] .... (listen) to music or play computer games.
My Mum [6] .... (take) us on trips at the weekends. We [7] .... (go) to the zoo, we visit a museum or we [8] .... (have) picnics.
[9] .... (your school/close) for a few days in the spring, too?
How [10] .... (you / spend) the holidays?
Love
Lucy

14 Tick (✔) the things you do in the holidays, and cross (✗) the things you don't do. Add more ideas.

How do you spend the holidays?		Do you ...?	
get up early	☐	get up late	☑
visit your friends	☐	go to school	☐
do homework	☐	read magazines	☐
listen to music	☐	play games with your best friend	☐
go to bed early	☐	go to bed late	☐
go shopping	☐	study for tests	☐
go on trips	☐	visit museums	☐

....
....
....

15 Write.

Write to *TeenLink* about how you spend the school holidays. Use Exercise 13 as a model.

How I spend the holidays

I love school holidays! I ....

....

....

....

8 Present simple, adverbs of frequency

1 **Complete the table.**

Adverbs of frequency		
always		I always have breakfast in the morning.
usually		I .... have cornflakes.
often		My mum .... makes pancakes.
sometimes		I .... have milk.
never		I .... eat fruit.

2 Read the information.

Adverbs of frequency

- We often use **adverbs of frequency** with the present simple to say how often something happens.
- Adverbs of frequency come before the main verb.
  Positive: *I **always** get up early.*
  Negative: *We don't **usually** go out on Fridays.*
  Question: *What do you **usually** do on Saturdays?*
- They come after the verb *be*.
  Positive: *We are **never** late for school.*
  Negative: *They aren't **usually** busy on Sundays.*
  Question: *Is your dad **always** tired after work?*

Time expressions

- **Time expressions** with more than one word come at the beginning or end of the sentence.
  ***Once a month** Jon visits his aunt.*
  *I meet my friends at the sports centre **three times a week.***
  *We go to the cinema **on Sundays**.*
  *I get up at 7.30 **every day**.*

3 Complete the questionnaire.

TeenLink

How healthy are you?

1 I eat breakfast in the morning.
A always B often C sometimes

2 I eat in a fast food restaurant.
A often B sometimes C never

3 I walk to school.
A usually B sometimes C never

4 I watch TV in my free time.
A always B usually C never

5 I have dinner after eight.
A always B sometimes C never

6 I go to bed early on weekdays.
A always B usually C never

4 Now write your answers to the questionnaire in Exercise 3.

1 I .... breakfast in the morning.
2 I .... in a fast food restaurant.
3 I .... to school.
4 I .... in my free time.
5 I .... after eight.
6 I .... on weekdays.

5 Complete.

1 Harry *doesn't always have* .... cornflakes for breakfast. (not have / always)
2 Peter and Lucy .... pancakes in the morning. (not eat / usually)
3 I .... late for school. (be / never)
4 My mum .... shopping on Fridays. (not go / always)
5 We .... jeans. (not wear / often)
6 Mrs Green .... busy on Saturdays. (not be / always)
7 In my country, it .... in the summer. (not rain / usually)
8 Sally .... late. (not get up / often)

6 Look and write questions and answers.

	always	usually	often	sometimes	never
Harry			walk to school		
Peter				eat fruit	
Beth					late for school
Lucy			go to the zoo		
Cosmo	eat a lot				
Izumi					get up late

1 Harry / walk to school / often?
Does Harry often walk to school? .... *Yes, he does.* ....
2 Peter / eat fruit / always?
Does Peter always eat fruit? .... *No, he sometimes. He never eats fruit.*
3 Beth / late for school / usually?
....
4 Lucy / go the zoo / often?
....
5 Cosmo / eat a lot / always?
....
6 Izumi / get up late / sometimes?
....

7 Put the expressions in the correct place.

1 I eat burgers. (never) *I never eat burgers.*
2 My brother eats burgers. (once a week) ....
3 My dad plays golf. (every weekend) ....
4 My mum plays tennis. (sometimes) ....
5 What time do you have lunch? (usually) ....
6 What time do you have supper? (on Saturdays) ....
7 Do you go to the sports centre? (often) ....
8 Does your brother go to the sports centre? (twice a week) ....

8 Read and complete.

A: What [1] do you usually do .... (do / usually) at weekends?
B: Well, lots of things. I go to the cinema with my cousin on Saturdays. And on Sundays, I [2] .... (visit / always) my grandparents.
A: [3] .... (you / visit / them / every week)?
B: Yes, I do.
A: And how often [4] .... (you / go) to the sports centre?
B: I [5] .... (go / never) to the sports centre. But my brother [6] .... (go / there / once a week). What about you? What [7] .... (you / do / on Sundays)?
A: I [8] .... (stay / usually) at home.
I [9] .... (watch / my favourite programme / in the morning) and then I [10] .... (do / my homework / in the afternoon).

Writing practice

9 Read, choose and write.

Dear Lucy,
It's Sunday today and I'm very happy. I [1] always .... (always / never) do all my homework on Saturday so I am free on Sunday.
I usually get up late [2] .... (at / on) Sunday mornings. I have breakfast and then I often play computer games with my brother, but I [3] .... (always / never) win!
I have lunch at home with my parents [4] .... (at / on) one o'clock. My mum is a fantastic cook!
My friend Keiko and I often go to the cinema [5] .... (in / on) the afternoon.
We [6] .... (sometimes / always) visit friends and we listen to music or chat.
[7] .... (At / In) the evening I watch TV with my family. Unfortunately, I [8] .... (usually / never) stay up late on a Sunday because Monday is a school day!
What about you? How do you spend your Sundays?
Love,
Izumi

10 Write.

Write to *TeenLink*. Tell us what you do on Sundays. Use Exercise 9 and the questions to help you.

I usually get up .... *on Sundays.*

I have breakfast and then I ....

....

....

....

1. *What time do you get up?*
2. *What do you do after breakfast?*
3. *Do you do your homework?*
4. *Where do you have lunch?*
5. *Do you meet your friends?*
6. *What do you do in the afternoon?*
7. *What do you do in the evening?*
8. *What time do you go to bed?*

Present continuous and present simple

Present continuous

1 **Complete the tables.**

Statements			
Positive	I	am ('m)	painting.
	We / You / They	are (.................)	
	He / She / It	is (.................)	
Negative	I	am not ('m not)	
	We / You / They	.... (aren't)	
	He / She / It	.... (isn't)	

▶ Look at the spelling rules on page 140.

Questions		
Am	....	painting?
....	we / you /	
....	he / she / it	

Short answers
Yes, I .... No, I'm not.
Yes, you / we / they are. No, you / we / they ....
Yes, he / she / it .... No, he / she / it isn't.

Wh- questions

Where	am	I	going?
What	are	you / we / they	doing?
Why	is	he / she / it	laughing?

2 Read the information.

Use

We use the **present continuous** to talk about:

- something that is happening now.
  Jenny is doing her homework.
- temporary situations:
  My cousins are staying with us this week.

Time expressions

- We often use these time expressions with the present continuous:
  now, right now, at the moment, today, this week/month/year, these days
  They're having dinner at the moment. (This is happening now.)
  Dad's working very hard these days.
  (This is happening for a short time only.)

3 Write the *-ing* form of the verbs in the correct column.

ask begin buy close dance drive leave open run
sit smile stop swim talk watch

-ing	*-e* + *-ing*	double consonant + *-ing*
asking	....	....
....	....	....
....	....	....
....	....	....
....	....	....

4 Complete with the present continuous.

1 It's Sunday and we *'re having* a barbecue in the garden. (have)
2 Dad .... steak on the barbecue. (cook)
3 Mum .... some sandwiches. (make)
4 Samantha .... photos with her new camera. (take)
5 Eric and Peter .... chess. (play)
6 Carol .... a letter to her new penfriend. (write)
7 Grandma and Grandpa .... under the tree. (sit)
8 The baby .... (sleep)
9 We .... a fantastic time! (have)
10 And I .... my new sunglasses today! (wear)

5 Look at the picture and correct the sentences.

1 Sonia is opening the door.
Sonia isn't opening the door. She's opening the window.
2 Maya is washing her face.
....
3 Liam and Dan are painting.
....
4 Lucy is talking to Sonia.
....
5 Tom and Alan are carrying a chair.
....
6 Keisha is writing in her notebook.
....
7 Sue is standing on a box.
....

Sonia
Liam
Dan
Sue
Lucy
Teacher
Keisha
Tom
Alan
Maya
Nick

6 Look at the picture in Exercise 5. Ask and answer.

1 Sonia / paint?
Is Sonia painting? No, she isn't.
2 Tom and Alan / talk / to the teacher?
....
3 Nick / drink / water?
....
4 Maya / wash / her brushes?
....
5 Keisha / open / the window?
....
6 Liam and Dan / eat?
....
7 Sue / stand / on a chair?
....

7 Complete with the present continuous.

A: Hi, Becky. This is Diane.
B: Oh, hi Diane. Where are you?
A: I'm at the sports centre with Sarah. We [1] 're playing (play) tennis. What [2] .... (you / do)?
B: I [3] .... (watch) a DVD.
A: Are your mum and dad there?
B: Yes. Mum [4] .... (make) the tea and Dad [5] .... (read) the paper. He [6] .... (not work) today.
A: Oh. What about your brother? Is [7] .... (he / play) the drums again?
B: No, he [8] .... He [9] .... (listen) to his new CD. And he [10] .... (dance)!

Present continuous and present simple

8 **Complete the tables.**

Present simple
He plays football every day. We stay at home on Sundays. She always .... breakfast at eight o'clock.
Time expressions
every day, on Sundays, at weekends, always, usually, sometimes, once a week

Present continuous
He .... playing football at the moment. We're .... at home today. She's having breakfast right now.
Time expressions
now, right now, at the moment, today, this week, these days

9 Read the information.

We use the **present simple**:

- for things that happen regularly.
  They watch TV every day.
- for things that are always or usually true.
  He works in London.

We use the **present continuous**:

- for things that are happening now.
  They're watching TV at the moment.
- for temporary situations.
  He's working in London this week.

Stative verbs

- We usually use the **present simple**, not the **present continuous**, for these verbs:
  believe, forget, hate, have (= have got), hear, know, like, love, need, remember, think, understand, want
  I like pop music. ✔
  ~~*I'm liking pop music.*~~
  What do you want? ✔
  ~~*What are you wanting?*~~

10 Look and write.

Every Monday afternoon | **Today**

1 Beth usually ...does... her homework on Monday afternoons. (do)
Today she ...'s going... to the dentist. (go)

2 Harry usually .... for *TeenLink* on Monday afternoons. (write)
Today he .... for a test. (study)

3 Peter and Lucy usually .... their rooms on Monday afternoons. (tidy)
Today they .... an art gallery. (visit)

4 Sophie usually .... the piano on Monday afternoons. (play)
Today she .... TV. (watch)

11 Complete with the present simple or present continuous.

1 Peter and Lucy ...are watching... TV at the moment. (watch)
2 We .... to the cinema every week. (not go)
3 The baby .... right now. (not sleep)
4 We usually .... our grandparents on Sundays. (visit)
5 What's that noise? .... the violin again? (Lucy / play)
6 Ben .... his new shoes today. (wear)
7 .... her room every day? (Emma / tidy)
8 .... today? (your father / work)
9 I .... my teeth three times a day. (brush)
10 .... the house on Saturdays? (your mother / clean)

12 **Complete the questions with one word. Write true answers.**

1 Do............ you live near your school? Yes, I do. / No, I don't.
2 Is............ your teacher speaking right now? Yes, she is. / No, she isn't.
3 .... your friends visit you on Sundays? ....
4 .... it raining at the moment? ....
5 .... your best friend speak French? ....
6 .... your teacher drive a car? ....
7 .... you listening to music? ....
8 .... you like pop music? ....

Writing practice

13 **Read and complete.**

Hi Izumi
Today is Sunday and I'm at home. My family and I usually [1]....go.......... (go) out for a meal on Sunday but not today. The weather is very good so we [2]................ (have) a barbecue in the garden! Our friends Harry and Beth are here, too. They usually [3]................ (spend) Sunday with their family but today they [4]................ (have) lunch with us.
At the moment, they're in the garden with Peter. They [5]................ (help) Dad with the barbeque. Mum [6]................ (wash) the salad and I [7]................ (make) the lemonade – well, I [8]................ (not make) it right now because I [9]................ (write) to you!
What [10]................ (you / do) today?
Love
Lucy

14 **Write.**

It's Wednesday and you are on holiday with your family. Write a postcard to a friend. Write about what you usually do on Wednesdays and what you are doing today. Use these ideas to help you.

Usually on Wednesdays	Today
have an English lesson	sit on the beach
visit my grandmother	swim
go to work	play handball
go to college	read a magazine

Hi ....!
Today is Wednesday. On Wednesdays, I usually ....
My mum usually ....
My dad ....
My brother/sister ....
But today we're on holiday! I ....
My mum ....
My dad ....
My brother/sister ....

10 -*ing* forms and infinitives

1 Complete the tables.

Verb + -*ing* as subject		
Shopping Skateboarding Cycl.........	is	fun. cool. my favourite sport.

like, love, hate + noun / -*ing* form		
I / You / We / They	like / love / hate	sport. shopping. computer games. paint ....
He / She / It	likes / loves / hates	

Adjective + preposition + noun / -*ing* form			
I	am	keen on interested in bored with good / bad at fond of crazy about	sport. computers. shopping. sing .... read......... magazines.
We / You / They	are		
He / She / It	is		

Infinitive	
I'd like I'd love I want	to buy these jeans. .... visit London. .... be a doctor.

▶ Look at the spelling rules on page 140.

2 Read the information.

-ing form
We use the **-ing form** of a verb like a noun:
- as the subject of a sentence:
  Swimming is my favourite sport.
- after adjectives with prepositions:
  Peter's not interested in shopping.
  I'm very bad at drawing.
- after the verbs *like*, *enjoy*, *love* and *hate*:
  I love dancing.
  I hate doing my homework!

Verbs followed by *to* + infinitive
We use *to* + the infinitive form of the verb after these verbs:
would like ('d like), would love ('d love), want.
I'd like to buy this T-shirt.
I don't want to go home.

3 Complete with the -*ing* form of the verb. Then circle *Yes* or *No*.

1 Skating ..... is great! (skate) Yes / No
2 .... is good for you. (swim) Yes / No
3 .... is fun. (fish) Yes / No
4 .... is good exercise. (walk) Yes / No
5 .... football is easy. (play) Yes / No
6 .... is dangerous! (ski) Yes / No
7 .... is very difficult. (surf) Yes / No
8 Bungee .... cool. (jump) Yes / No

Look!
When we add -*ing* to some verbs, the spelling changes:
dance ➜ *dancing*
swim ➜ *swimming*

4 Look and write. Then complete the table and write about you.

☺ = like ☺☺ = love ☹ = hate

	play chess	listen to music	do sport	dance
Diane	☹	☺☺	☺	☺
Steve	☺	☺	☺☺	☹
Me	....	....	....	....

1 Diane / play chess Diane hates playing chess.
2 Steve / listen to music ....
3 Diane / do sport ....
4 Steve / dance ....
5 Diane / listen to music ....
6 Steve / do sport ....
7 I / dance ....
8 I / play chess ....

5 Write questions and true answers.

1 you / like / do sport?
Do you like doing sport? .... Yes, I do. / No, I don't.

2 you / enjoy / learn English?
....

3 your friends / like / cycle?
....

4 you / hate / visit museums?
....

5 your friends / enjoy / write emails?
....

6 your mum / like / shop?
....

7 your dad / like / swim?
....

8 you / enjoy / go to the park?
....

6 Choose and write. Then put a tick (✔) or cross (✗) in the box. Correct the false sentences.

~~at~~ about at in of ~~on~~ on with

1 My friends are very keen on.......... playing computer games. ✔
....

2 I'm good at......... drawing. ✗
Wrong. I'm bad at drawing.

3 My cousin's interested .... studying History. ☐
....

4 I'm bad .... writing stories. ☐
....

5 My best friend is crazy .... cooking. ☐
....

6 I'm not very fond .... painting. ☐
....

7 I'm very keen .... learning about computers. ☐
....

8 I'm bored .... watching cartoons on TV. ☐
....

7 Read, choose and complete.

~~buy~~ have work be stay go do visit

1 I'd like to buy...... these jeans, please.
2 I'd love .... camping in the holidays.
3 I want .... a doctor.
4 I don't want .... in an office.
5 My brother would love .... New York.
6 My mum wants .... a new car.
7 My brother doesn't want .... his homework.
8 My friend and I would like .... up late every night.

8 Circle the correct words.

1 A: I hate to shop / shopping! I think it's boring.
  B: I love it!
2 A: I want to be / being a doctor.
  B: Me, too!
3 A: Let's get a camera for Nick's birthday.
  B: Great idea! He loves to take / taking photos.
4 A: Anna's pictures are fantastic!
  B: Yes, she's really good at to paint / painting.
5 A: I'd like to live / living in London.
  B: Really? I hate big cities.
6 A: Do you enjoy to go / going to the cinema?
  B: Yes. Peter and I go every Saturday.
7 A: I'd love to come / coming with you.
  B: Great! Let's go, then!
8 A: I don't want to wear / wearing this dress.
  B: But you look beautiful in it!

Writing practice

9 Read, choose and write.

TeenLink

E-Friends

Luciano is thirteen years old and he lives in Rome.

He's very good at [1] .... friends and [2] .... jokes. He [3] .... playing football and he wants [4] .... a professional footballer one day. He also enjoys [5] .... model planes. Luciano [6] .... going to the dentist and getting up early at the weekends. He [7] .... to visit the UK with his parents in the summer. He'd like [8] .... emails in English for practice

1 a) make	b) to make	c) making
2 a) to tell	b) telling	c) tell
3 a) loving	b) loves	c) 'd love
4 a) to be	b) being	c) be
5 a) fly	b) flying	c) is flying
6 a) hates	b) 'd like	c) wants to
7 a) love	b) 'd love	c) 's good at
8 a) writing	b) 'd write	c) to write

10 Write.

Write a paragraph for *TeenLink*'s 'E-Friends'. Use Exercise 9 as a model.

My name is .... I'm .... old
and I live ....
I'm very good at .... and ....
I love .... I want to be ....
....
I hate .... and ....
I'd love to .... I'd like to ....

Use your English (Units 6–10)

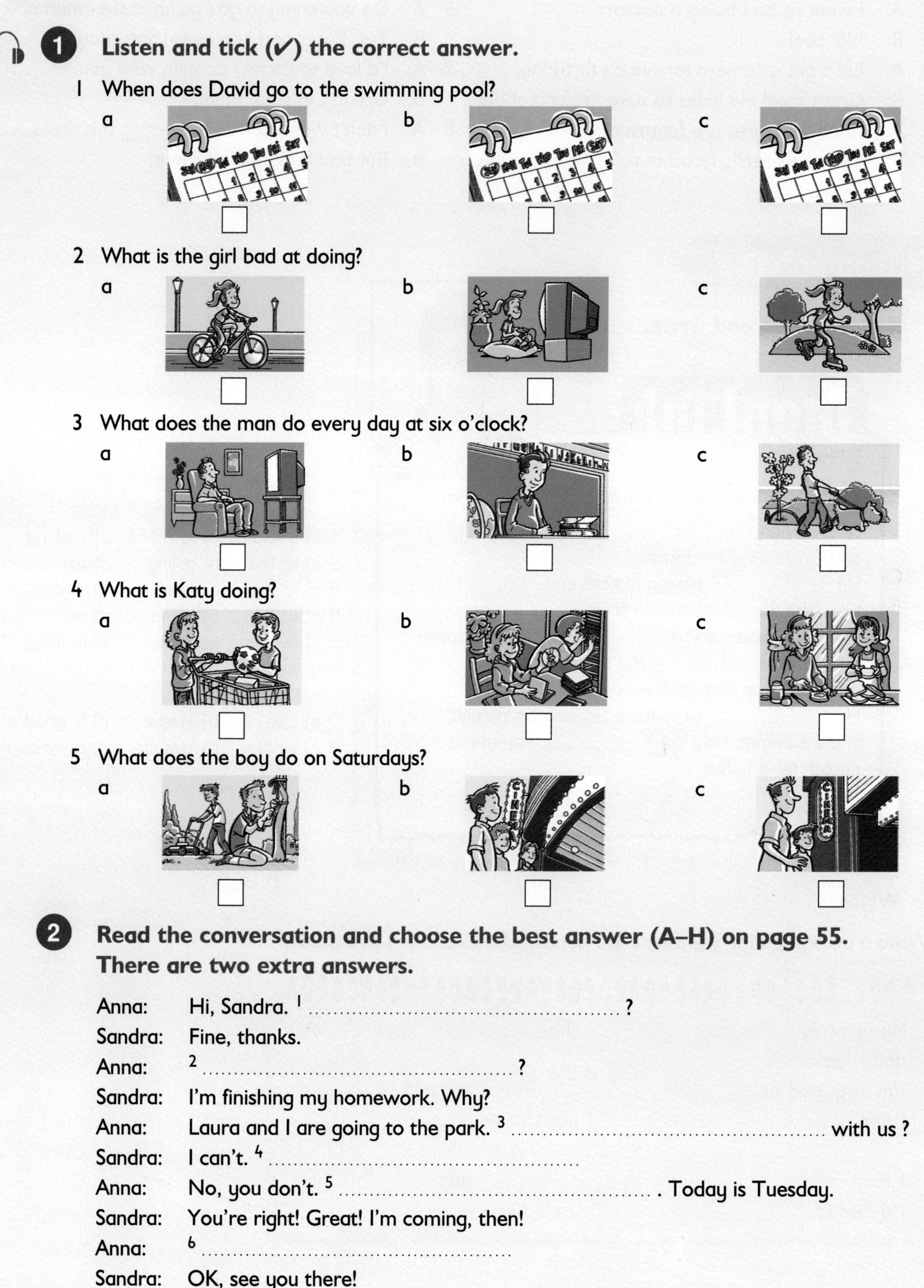

1 Listen and tick (✓) the correct answer.

1 When does David go to the swimming pool?

a ☐ b ☐ c ☐

2 What is the girl bad at doing?

a ☐ b ☐ c ☐

3 What does the man do every day at six o'clock?

a ☐ b ☐ c ☐

4 What is Katy doing?

a ☐ b ☐ c ☐

5 What does the boy do on Saturdays?

a ☐ b ☐ c ☐

2 Read the conversation and choose the best answer (A–H) on page 55. There are two extra answers.

Anna: Hi, Sandra. [1] .... ?

Sandra: Fine, thanks.

Anna: [2] .... ?

Sandra: I'm finishing my homework. Why?

Anna: Laura and I are going to the park. [3] .... with us ?

Sandra: I can't. [4] ....

Anna: No, you don't. [5] .... Today is Tuesday.

Sandra: You're right! Great! I'm coming, then!

Anna: [6] ....

Sandra: OK, see you there!

Anna: Bye!

A Your piano lesson is on Wednesdays
B Do you want to come
C You're coming
D How are you
E What do you do
F I have a piano lesson at four o'clock
G What are you doing right now
H Let's meet at Laura's

3 Read Sandra's story. Complete the sentences about the story. Use 1–4 words.

On Sundays my brother George and I usually visit our Granny with our parents. She lives in a house with a small garden. We have lunch together and then we all go for a walk if the weather is nice. Granny loves cooking and she always has a special cake for us to take home. Ginger, Granny's cat, loves sitting under the table because my brother and I give her food when Granny isn't looking. Ginger loves food but Granny says that she is a little fat and that she must only eat her cat food.

1 Sandra usually spends Sundays *with her Granny*.
2 Granny's house has ....
3 On warm, sunny days they all .... after lunch.
4 Granny always gives them .... when they leave.
5 The name of Sandra's Granny's cat is ....
6 Sandra and her brother mustn't .... because she is a little fat.

4 Write full answers to the questions about you.

1 What do you usually do on Saturday morning?
....
2 What do you usually eat for breakfast?
....
3 What do you never do on Sunday?
....
4 What are you doing at the moment?
....
5 When is your birthday?
....
6 What do you love doing in your free time?
....
7 What do you hate doing when you're tired?
....
8 What are you good/bad at?
....

Now you can ...

✔ Talk about habits and routines:
I do my homework every day.
School starts at 8.30.

✔ Talk about what is happening now:
They're playing football.
I'm having lunch.

✔ Use different time expressions:
I usually get up early.
It's cold in winter.
Her birthday is on the 7th of May.
They play tennis every afternoon.

✔ Use a gerund or the infinitive:
Swimming is good for you.
I love listening to music.
We'd like to visit Italy.

11 Countable and uncountable nouns, *some* / *any* / *no*

1 **Complete the table.**

	Plural countable nouns	Uncountable nouns
Positive	There .... some bananas in the bowl.	There .... some yoghurt in the fridge.
Negative	There .... any bananas in the bowl. There are no bananas in the bowl.	There isn't any yoghurt in the fridge. There's no yoghurt in the fridge.
Questions	.... there any bananas in the bowl?	.... there any yoghurt in the fridge?

2 Read the information.

Countable and uncountable nouns

- **Countable nouns** can be singular or plural. We can count them:
  one apple two apples three apples
- **Uncountable nouns** have no plural form. We can't count them:
  yoghurt milk water cheese money
  ~~one milk~~ - ~~two milks~~

a/an, some, any, no

- We use ***a/an*** with singular countable nouns. We use ***some***, ***any*** and ***no*** (= *not any*) with plural countable nouns and uncountable nouns.
- We use ***some*** in positive sentences.
  There are some apples in that bowl.
  There's some milk in the fridge.
- We use ***any*** in negative sentences and questions.
  There aren't any apples in that bowl.
  There isn't any milk in the fridge.
  Are there any apples in that bowl?
  Is there any milk in the fridge?
- ***No*** means 'not one' or 'not any'. We use it with positive verbs.
  There are no apples in that bowl.
  (= *There aren't any apples in that bowl.*)
  There's no milk in the fridge.
  (= *There isn't any milk in the fridge.*)

3 Write the words in the correct column.

~~apples~~ biscuit bottles bread can cheese children coffee egg feet knife meat mice poster sandwiches table tea ~~yoghurt~~

Countable nouns		Uncountable nouns
Singular	Plural	
....	*apples*	*yoghurt* ....
....	....	....
....	....	....
....	....	....
....	....	....
....	....	....

4 Complete with *a* or *some*.

Peter and Harry are at a takeaway.

Assistant: What would you like?
Peter: I'd like [1] *a*.............. burger and [2] .... fries, please.
Harry: I'd like [3] .... cheese sandwich.
Assistant: And to drink?
Peter: I'd like [4] .... orange juice, please.
Harry: And I'd like [5] .... can of cola, please.
Assistant: Anything else?
Harry: Yes. I'd like [6] .... popcorn, please.
Peter: And I'd like [7] .... bar of chocolate.
Oh, and [8] .... chocolate biscuits.

5 What's in the picture? Look and complete.

1 There *are some* .... biscuits on the table.
2 There .... yoghurt in the pot.
3 There .... cats at the window.
4 There .... mice at the window.
5 There .... popcorn in the box.
6 There .... chocolate on the table.
7 There .... chips on the table.
8 There .... bananas in the bowl.

6 Look at the picture in Exercise 5 for a minute. Then cover the picture. Write questions and answers.

1 biscuits
Are there any biscuits? .... *Yes, there are.* ....

2 popcorn
....

3 bananas
....

4 milk
....

5 sandwiches
....

6 yoghurt
....

7 burgers
....

8 water
....

7 Circle the correct answer.

1 There isn't (any) / no yoghurt in the fridge.
2 There are any / no bananas in the bowl.
3 There's any / no cola in this bottle.
4 There isn't any / no sugar in my tea.
5 We haven't got any / no CDs for the party.
6 There are any / no children in the park today.
7 I can't see any / no clouds in the sky.
8 Well done! There are any / no mistakes in your test!

something / anything / nothing

8 **Complete the table.**

	People	Things	Places
Positive	There's **someone** there.	There's **something** in this box.	They're going ....**where**.
Negative & Questions	There isn't **anyone** there. Is there ....**body** there?	There isn't ....**thing** in this box. Is there **anything** in this box?	They aren't going **anywhere**. Are they going ....**where?**
Negative	There's **no-one** there.	There's **nothing** in this box.	They're going ....**where**.

9 Read the information.

- We use ***someone*** (or ***somebody***), ***anyone*** (or ***anybody***) and ***no-one*** (or ***nobody***) to talk about people.
  There's somebody/someone downstairs.
  There's nobody/no one downstairs.
- We use ***something***, ***anything*** and ***nothing*** to talk about things.
  There's something in this box.
  Is there anything in this box?
  There's nothing in the fridge.
- We use ***somewhere***, ***anywhere*** and ***nowhere*** to talk about places.
  They're going somewhere. We're going nowhere.
- We use ***some-*** and ***no-*** in positive sentences.
  There's somebody/someone in the room.
  There's nobody/no-one in the room.
- We use ***any-*** in negative sentences and questions.
  There isn't anything in this bag.
  Is there anything in this bag?

10 Circle the correct answer.

1 Dad, there's someone / anyone here to see you.

2 I can't go anywhere / nowhere tonight!

3 There's anything / nothing in the fridge.

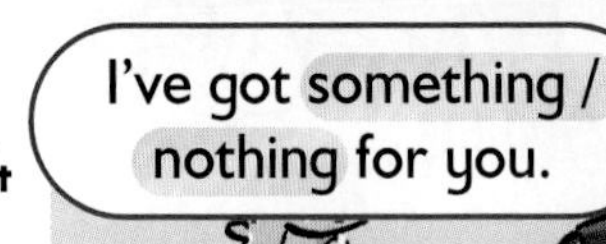

4 I've got something / nothing for you.

5 Is there something / anything in that bag?

6 There's anyone / no-one here!

11 Choose and complete.

anyone anything anywhere no-one nothing ~~someone~~ something somewhere

1 Listen! Someone's in the house!
2 Come here. I want to tell you ....
3 Does .... know the answer to this question?
4 There's .... in this bag. It's empty.
5 I can't find my sunglasses ....!
6 There's .... in the kitchen. They are all in the garden.
7 No, I can't buy ....! I haven't got any money.
8 My cousin lives .... near Cambridge.

12 Read and write true answers.

1 Is there any fruit in your schoolbag?
No, there isn't any fruit in my schoolbag. / Yes, there are two apples in my schoolbag.
2 Are there any sweets in your kitchen at home?
....
3 Is there anything on your desk?
....
4 Have you got anything in your pocket?
....
5 Is there anyone at your house at the moment?
....
6 Does anyone in your family speak Chinese?
....

Writing practice

13 Complete with one word.

Jessica: I'm hungry and there's [1] *nothing* in the fridge!
George: Well, we can cook [2] .... ! Let's make some pancakes!
Jessica: Have you got a recipe?
George: Yes, here it is. We need some milk, some eggs, some flour and some sugar.
Jessica: Have we got [3] .... milk?
George: Yes, there's [4] .... milk in the fridge.
Jessica: Have we got [5] .... flour?
George: Yes, there's [6] .... flour in that tin.
Jessica: No, there isn't. There's [7] .... in it. It's empty!
George: Oh, no! Now we can't make pancakes!
Jessica: Listen! There's [8] .... at the kitchen door. Oh, it's Mum.
Mum: Hello, you two! Are you hungry? I've got [9] .... doughnuts for you!

PANCAKES
milk
eggs
flour
sugar

14 Write.

You and your friend are hungry. Look at the recipe and write a dialogue.
Use Exercise 13 as a model.

FAIRY CAKES
125 grams butter
125 grams sugar
125 grams flour
2 eggs
15 ml milk

You: *Let's make* ....
We need ....
Your friend: *Have we got* ....
....
....
....

Quantity: *much*, *many*, *a lot of*

1 **Complete the table.**

	Plural countable nouns			Uncountable nouns		
Positive	We've got a lot of hot dogs.			We've got a lot .... cola.		
Negative	We haven't got	.... lot of many	hot dogs.	We haven't got	a lot of much	cola.
Questions	Have we got	a lot of many	hot dogs?	Have we got	a lot of much	cola?
	How .... hot dogs have we got?			.... much cola have we got?		

2 Read the information.

Countable and uncountable nouns

- We can make uncountable nouns countable. We use the container or the quantity. We say: *a bottle of water, a can of cola, a carton of milk, a loaf of bread, a slice of pizza, a kilo of flour,* etc.

a lot of

- We use ***a lot of*** with countable and uncountable nouns to talk about a large number or a large quantity.
  There are a lot of apples in that bag. There aren't a lot of oranges in that bowl.
  There's a lot of food in the fridge.
  Is there a lot of cola in that bottle?

(not) much, (not) many

- We use ***not much*** and ***not many*** in negative sentences to talk about a small number or a small quantity. We use ***not much*** with uncountable nouns and ***not many*** with plural countable nouns.
  I haven't got much money.
  There aren't many shops here.

We can use ***much*** and ***many*** in questions.
Have you got much money?
Are there many shops in this town?

How much? How many?

- To ask about quantities, we use ***how much*** and ***how many***. We use ***how much*** with uncountable nouns and ***how many*** with countable nouns.
  A: *How many cans of cola has he got?*
  B: *Two.*
  A: *How much bread do we need?*
  B: *Three loaves.*
- We often use ***a lot*** in positive short answers and ***not much/not many*** in negative short answers.
  A: *How much milk do we need?*
  B: *A lot!*
  A: *How much money have you got?*
  B: *Not much.*
  A: *How many cinemas are there in this town?*
  B: *Not many.*

3 Match and draw lines.

1 a carton of
2 a tin of
3 a slice of
4 a bottle of
5 a kilo of
6 a bar of
7 a loaf of
8 a can of

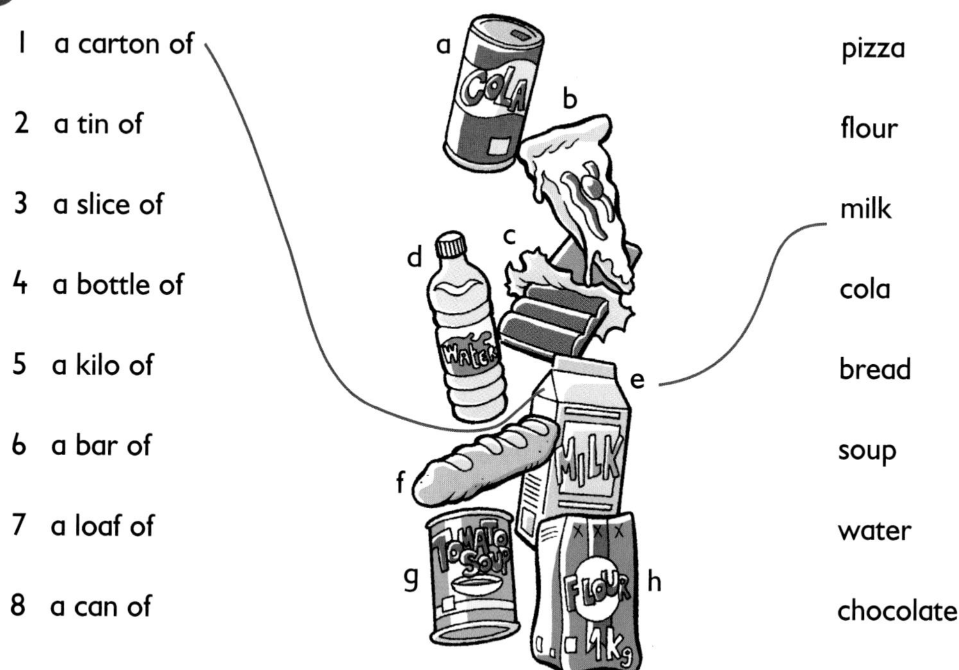

pizza
flour
milk
cola
bread
soup
water
chocolate

4 Look, count and write.

bottles bars packet ~~cartons~~ tins kilos cans loaves

I'm hungry! What have we got here? There are [1] *two cartons* .... of milk, and [2] .... of orange juice. There's [3] .... of sugar and [4] .... of cola. There are [5] .... of flour and [6] .... of soup – yuck! There are [7] .... of chocolate, and [8] .... of bread but there's NO CAT FOOD! Help!

5 Circle the correct answer.

1 We've got (a lot of) / many food in the fridge.
2 Are there a lot of / much people in the park today?
3 There isn't much / many milk in Cosmo's bowl.
4 There aren't much / many biscuits in that packet.
5 There isn't a lot of / many apple juice in the fridge.
6 I haven't got much / many money.
7 Hurry up! We haven't got a lot of / many time.
8 Are there much / many cinemas in your town?
9 Do much / a lot of tourists come here in the summer?
10 Have you got a lot of / many homework?

6 Complete with *How much* or *How many*. Then circle the correct answer.

1 A: .... pancakes can you eat? B: Not much. / A lot!
2 A: .... popcorn have we got? B: Not much. / Not many.
3 A: .... eggs do you need for the omelette? B: Three. / Not much.
4 A: .... sugar do you take in your tea? B: Not many. / A lot!
5 A: .... cheeseburgers have you got? B: Not much. / Not many.
6 A: .... cans of cola are there in the fridge? B: Six. / Not much.
7 A: .... water is there in that bottle? B: A litre. / Not many.
8 A: .... juice have we got? B: Not much. / Not many.
9 A: .... bags of crisps do you want? B: Eight. / Not much.
10 A: .... sandwiches do we need for the party? B: Not much. / A lot!

7 Read and complete.

Harry: Angela, I'm doing a Healthy Eating report for *TeenLink*. Can I ask you some questions about your diet?

Angela: Yes, of course.

Harry: How [1] .... red meat do you eat?

Angela: Not [2] .... But I eat a [3] .... of fish and chicken.

Harry: Do you eat [4] .... biscuits?

Angela: No, not [5] .... Biscuits have [6] .... lot of sugar.

Harry: What about fruit and vegetables?

Angela: I eat three or four pieces [7] .... fruit every day. I love fruit! And I eat vegetables with every meal.

Harry: How [8] .... litres of water do you drink?

Angela: I drink about two [9] .... of water every day.

Harry: Thanks, Angela.

Writing practice

8 Read, look and complete.

TeenLink

I think my diet is healthy. I eat two [1] *pieces* of fruit every day and I drink [2] .... orange juice with my lunch. I don't eat [3] .... fish because I don't like it. I usually eat chicken and red meat. Fortunately I love vegetables. I eat [4] .... vegetables with every meal. I don't eat [5] .... chocolate and I only have one [6] .... of cake in the afternoon. I drink [7] .... water every day and [8] .... of cola.

Adrian, 12

9 Write.

Write to *TeenLink* about your diet. Say how much you eat and drink of the things in the list. Use Exercise 8 as a model.

I think my diet is ....

....

....

....

pizza fruit water
sweets vegetables milk
chocolate chicken cola
biscuits fish orange juice

13 *was, were*

1 **Complete the tables.**

Statements			
Positive	I / He / She / It	was	at home.
	You / We / They	were	asleep.
Negative	I / He / She / It	was .... (wasn't)	at home.
	You / We / They	.... not (weren't)	asleep.

Questions		
Was	I / he / she / it	at home? asleep?
Were	you / we / they	

Short answers
Yes, I / he / she / it .... No, I / he / she / it wasn't.
Yes, you / we / they were. No, you / we / they ....

Wh- questions			
Why	was	I / he / she / it	late?
When	....	you / we / they	asleep?

2 Read the information.

was* / *were

- ***was* / *were*** is the past simple form of *be*. We use it to talk about the past.
- We often use these time expressions when we talk about the past:

  yesterday:
  Lizzie was very busy yesterday.
  last night/week/month/year:
  I wasn't at home last night.
  five minutes/days/months ago:
  Matt was here five minutes ago.

There was* / *There were

- The past simple of ***There is* / *There are*** is ***There was* / *There were***.

  There were a lot of people at the cinema.
  There weren't any phone calls for you.
  A: Were there any phone calls for me?
  B: No, there weren't.

3 Complete the sentences with *was* or *were*. Are the sentences true for you? Put a tick (✓) or cross (✗) in the box.

1 I was / were in the school football team last year. ☐
2 I was / were in the park at the weekend. ☐
3 It was / were very hot here last week. ☐
4 My friends was / were all at my house last night. ☐
5 My family and I was / were on holiday two weeks ago. ☐
6 My mum was / were very busy yesterday. ☐
7 My dad was / were at work last week. ☐
8 My friends and I was / were at school yesterday. ☐

4 Where were they yesterday afternoon? Look at the table and correct the sentences.

Yesterday afternoon ...			
Peter	at the sports centre	Cosmo and Bella	in the garden
Lucy	at home	Mr and Mrs Hardy	at the theatre
Harry	in the library	Aunt Agatha	at the hairdresser's
Beth	at the dentist's		

1 Peter was at school.
Wrong! *He wasn't at school. He was at the sports centre.*
2 Lucy was at the cinema.
Wrong! ....
3 Harry was at the shops.
Wrong! ....
4 Beth was at school.
Wrong! ....
5 Cosmo and Bella were at the park.
Wrong! ....
6 Mr and Mrs Hardy were at the cinema.
Wrong! ....
7 Aunt Agatha was at the theatre.
Wrong! ....

5 Write questions. Then complete the short answers.

1 you / at home yesterday afternoon?
A: Were you at home yesterday afternoon? B: No, I wasn't.
2 you / at the cinema?
A: .... B: Yes, ...
3 Mick and Carol / with you?
A: .... B: No, ...
4 they / at the sports centre?
A: .... B: Yes, ...
5 the film / good?
A: .... B: No, ...
6 it / a comedy?
A: .... B: Yes, ...
7 your brother / at home?
A: .... B: No, ...
8 he / at the sports centre, too?
A: .... B: Yes, ...

Look!
When were you in London? ✔
~~*When you were in London?*~~

6 Put the words in the correct order. Then write true answers.

1 yesterday morning / you / where / were ?
Where were you yesterday morning? ....
2 you / were / old / how / two years ago ?
....
3 last night / were / your / where / parents ?
....
4 on / your family / were / holiday / last year / you / when / and ?
....
5 why / you / sad / last week / were ?
....
6 time / what / best friend / school / this morning / at / your / was ?
....

7 Read about Kim's mum's school. Circle the correct words.

[1] There wasn't / There weren't many pupils at my mum's school. [2] There was / There were eight boys and six girls in her class. [3] There wasn't / There weren't a swimming pool at the school. And [4] there wasn't / there weren't a cafeteria. [5] There was / There were a small gym. And [6] there was / there were a small library. But [7] there wasn't / there weren't any computers in the library.

8 Read, choose and write.

Lyn:	Where [1] *were you* last Saturday?	1 a) you were	b) you was	(c) were you)
Tony:	[2]................ at the school party.	2 a) Was	b) I was	c) I were
Lyn:	[3]................ with you, too?	3 a) Mark was	b) Was Mark	c) Were Mark
Tony:	No, he [4]................ . He was at home.	4 a) was	b) wasn't	c) were
Lyn:	[5]................ many people at the party?	5 a) Were there	b) There were	c) Were they
Tony:	I don't know. About twenty, I think. [6]................ were with me, too.	6 a) Jo and Pat	b) Jo	c) Pat
Lyn:	Really? So, [7]................ a good party?	7 a) Was it	b) Was there	c) There was
Tony:	No. [8]................ terrible! The music was awful and the food [9]................ very good.	8 a) Was	b) It was	c) It were
		9 a) not	b) wasn't	c) weren't

Writing practice

9 Read and complete with the correct form of the verb *be*.

TeenLink

This is a picture of our town one hundred years ago!

It [1] *was*......... a quiet little town. There [2]................ any cars in the street. There [3] .... only horses and carriages. The air [4] .... clean and there [5] .... a lot of trees.

There [6] .... many shops in High Street, only a bakery, a greengrocer's and a teashop. Postmen [7] .... very busy! Their bags [8] .... full of letters. There [9] .... any computers or emails or mobile phones then. There [10] .... only three telephones in the whole town!

10 Write.

Write to *TeenLink* about your town or village one hundred years ago.
Answer the questions. Use Exercise 9 as a model.

My town was a quiet little town a hundred years ago. There .... many cars in the street. ....

....

....

....

Were there many cars in the street?
Were there a lot of trees?
What shops were there in the High Street?
Were there any computers?
Were there any mobile phones?

14 Past simple

Regular verbs

It's a crazy world!

TELEPHONE
In June 2008, John Smith talked to 146 people on the phone for 70 hours without stopping!
1

On September 6th 2007, Bettina Rossi baked a cake for her birthday. It weighed 170 kilos and she invited the whole village to eat it!
HAPPY BIRTHDAY
2

Four months ago, Jamal Keyes played for his school basketball team for the first time and scored 102 points in one game!
3

Last year, Paul and Emma Yates travelled round Europe and Asia on their bikes. They visited 28 countries in five months!
4

1 **Complete the tables.**

Past simple regular verbs

Statements			
Positive	I / You / He / She / It / We / They	played. travelled. talk......... .	
Negative	I / You / He / She / It / We / They	did .... (didn't)	play. .... talk.

Questions		
Did	I / you / he / she / it / we / they	play? travel? ....?

Short answers
Yes, I / you / he / she / it / we / they did. No, I / you / he / she / it / we / they ....

▶ Look at the spelling rules on page 141.

Wh- questions			
What Where When	did	I / you / he / she / it / we / they	play? travel? ....?

2 Read the information.

Use

- We use the **past simple** to talk about things that happened in the past. We usually say when they happened. We often use past time expressions:
  We walked to school yesterday.
  She finished her homework an hour ago.

Form

- To form the past simple of regular verbs, we add *-ed* or *-d* to the main verb:
  play ➜ *played* *like* ➜ *liked*
  tidy ➜ *tidied* *stop* ➜ *stopped*
- In negative sentences and questions, we use ***didn't/did*** and the infinitive.
  Did you play football yesterday? ✔

3 Complete with the past simple.

TeenLink

Amazing facts

In February 2004, a young man from Australia.[1] played........ (play) the drums for 84 hours.
The largest sandwich in the world [2] .... (weigh) 2,467 kg.
Sergio Goldvarg of Argentina [3] .... (collect) 7000 model cars in 43 years (1962–2005).
In 2000, a 34-year-old man from Nepal [4] .... (climb) Mount Everest in 16 hours and 56 minutes!
In 1930, Mike Ritof and Edith Boudreaux [5] .... (dance) for 5152 hours and 48 minutes.
Pelé, one of the world's greatest football players, [6] .... (score) 1280 goals in 1360 games!

4 Correct the sentences.

1 Harry watched a film on TV last night.
He didn't watch a film. He watched cartoons.

2 Beth and Vicky played football on Saturday.
.... tennis.

3 You studied for your Maths test last weekend.
I .... History test.

4 Mrs Hardy baked a chocolate cake last Sunday.
.... a banana cake.

5 Lucy phoned Izumi yesterday.
.... Sophie.

5 Look and write. Use the past simple.

1 Peter / tidy / his room
Peter didn't tidy his room.

2 Sophie / help / her teacher
Sophie helped her teacher.

3 Harry / finish / his puzzle
....

4 Lucy / play the violin
....

5 Beth / cook / spaghetti
....

6 Mr Hardy / go / to work
....

6 Look at Exercise 5. Ask and answer.

1 Peter / tidy / the living room / yesterday?
Did Peter tidy the living room yesterday? No he didn't.

2 Harry / finish his puzzle?
....

3 Beth / cook / fish?
....

4 Lucy / play / the violin?
....

5 Sophie / help / her teacher?
....

6 Mr Hardy / stay / in bed?
....

7 Choose and complete with the correct form of the past simple.

visit ~~enjoy~~ stay talk

Harry's friend, Leo, visited Spain last month.

Harry: 1 Did you enjoy your holiday in Spain?
Leo: Yes, I 2 .... It was great.
Harry: 3 .... in a hotel?
Leo: No, we 4 .... We stayed at my uncle's house.
Harry: 5 .... to any local people?
Leo: No, I 6 .... I don't speak Spanish.
Harry: 7 .... the Alhambra in Granada?
Leo: Yes, I 8 .... It was fantastic!

Irregular verbs

8 **Complete the tables.**

Past simple regular verbs

Statements			
Positive	I / You / He / She / It / We / They	saw. ate. wrote.	
Negative	I / You / He / She / It / We / They	did .... (didn't)	see. eat. ....

Questions		
Did	I / you / he / she / it / we / they	see? ....? write?

Short answers
Yes, I / you / he / she / it / we / they did. No, I / you / he / she / it / we / they ....

***Wh-* questions**			
What Where When	did	I / you / he / she / it / we / they	eat?

9 Read the information.

- **Irregular verbs** don't form the past simple with *-ed*. Each irregular verb is different.
  go ➔ *went* *see* ➔ *saw* *eat* ➔ *ate* *write* ➔ *wrote*
  We went the supermarket. We didn't go to the supermarket. Did you go out?

▶ See the list of irregular verbs on page 138.

10 Match.

Infinitive	Past simple
1 wear	a ran
2 think	b swam
3 run	c drank
4 give	d had
5 swim	e found
6 take	f wore
7 drink	g sang
8 find	h did
9 make	i thought
10 sing	j took
11 have	k made
12 do	l gave

11 Complete with the past simple.

1 Peter and Harry ...saw... Ben Baker at the supermarket. (see)
2 They .... his autograph. (get)
3 I .... a letter to my friend in Spain. (write)
4 We .... our homework and then we watched TV. (do)
5 My mum .... a cake for my birthday. (make)
6 Hey! You .... my sandwich! (eat)
7 David .... a present for his friend yesterday. (buy)
8 I .... a very interesting book last week. (read)

12 Read Peter's list of things to do on Saturday. What did he do? What didn't he do?

Saturday
get up at 8.00! ✔
do my homework for Monday ✔
tell Mum about the concert ✔
get tickets for the concert ✗
buy some cat food for Cosmo and Bella ✗
send an email to David ✗
meet Harry (5.30) ✔

1 *He got up at 8.00.* ....
2 ....
3 ....
4 ....
5 ....
6 ....
7 ....

13 Complete the questions. Then write short answers. Don't look at Exercise 12. How much can you remember?

1 Did Peter get up .... at 8.00 on Saturday? (Peter / get up) Yes, he did.
2 .... his homework for Monday? (he / do) ....
3 .... his mum about the concert? (he / tell) ....
4 .... tickets for the concert? (he / get) ....
5 .... any cat food? (he / buy) ....
6 .... an email to David? (he / send) ....
7 .... Harry at half past five? (he / meet) ....

14 Complete.

Dear Izumi,

I had an awful time yesterday! I ¹ went (go) to the leisure centre with Peter in the morning. I ² .... (forget) my swimsuit so I ³ .... (not go) swimming.

Then we played volleyball with some kids from school. Our team ⁴ .... (not win) because Peter was a terrible player! After the game I ⁵ .... (break) my sunglasses and then I ⁶ .... (lose) my i-pod!

We ⁷ .... (come) back home at four o'clock and ⁸ .... (find) Mum outside our house. She ⁹ .... (not have) her keys so we all ¹⁰ .... (wait) for Dad in the garden. He ¹¹ .... (come) back from work after two hours!

Love,

Lucy

15 Read Exercise 14 again and answer the questions.

1 Where did Lucy go yesterday morning? She went to the leisure centre.
2 Did she have a good time? No, she didn't.
3 Why didn't she swim? ....
4 Did Lucy's team win the volleyball game? ....
5 What happened to her sunglasses? ....
6 Why did they wait for their dad in the garden? ....
7 When did he come home from work? ....

All forms

16 Complete with the past simple.

Every summer ...	Last summer ...
1 I go on holiday with my family.	we *went* to Spain.
2 we travel by plane.	we .... by train.
3 we stay in a hotel.	we .... in a small hotel near the beach.
4 I get up late.	I .... at ten o'clock every morning.
5 my brother and I swim in the sea.	we .... in the hotel swimming pool.
6 we meet a lot of new people.	we .... a very nice family with two children.
7 I send a postcard to my best friend.	I .... postcards to all my friends.
8 we visit my grandparents in August.	we .... my grandparents in July.

17 Complete with the past simple.

A: What [1] *did you do* (you / do) last weekend? [2]......................... (you / stay) at home?

B: No, we [3].......................... We [4]......................... (visit) my cousins in Brighton.

A: Really? [5]......................... (you / have) a nice time?

B: Yes! It [6]......................... (be) lovely! What about you? Where [7] .... (you / go)?

A: Well I [8]......................... (go) to the shopping centre with Mike and Nancy on Saturday. And guess what? We [9]......................... (see) Ray Matthews there!

B: Ray Matthews? The famous footballer? Wow! [10] .... (you / speak) to him?

A: Yes, I [11]......................... ! And I [12]......................... (get) his autograph, too. Here it is.

18 What did you do last weekend? Write questions. Then write true answers.

1 what time / you / get up / last Saturday?
What time did you get up last Saturday? ... *I got up at ten o'clock.*

2 you / go / shopping with a friend?
....

3 what / you / do / in the afternoon?
....

4 a friend / call / you?
....

5 where / you / go / on Sunday?
....

6 you / stay / at home?
....

7 you / do / any homework?
....

8 what time / you / go / to bed?
....

Writing practice

19 **Choose and complete with the correct form of the past simple.**

leave fly know take ~~meet~~ play talk want visit ask

TeenLink

NBA basketball star in our town!

by Harry Davis

Ben Baker, the famous NBA basketball player, was in our town last week! I [1] *met* .... Ben at a local supermarket and I [2] .... him for his autograph. Then I [3] .... to him about his visit.
Ben [4] .... to England last week because he [5] .... to visit his relatives. [6] .... you .... that Ben's grandparents live in our town? I didn't!

Ben has many fans in our town. Last Wednesday he [7] .... the sports centre and [8] .... a game with the local basketball team.
Ben [9] .... for the USA yesterday, but he wants to come back and visit our school very soon! Sadly, I didn't [10] .... a photo of Ben.

20 **Write.**

You met a famous person in your town last week. Write an article for *TeenLink* about this person. Use Exercise 19 and these questions to help you.

FAMOUS .... IN OUR TOWN!

by ....

................................, the famous ....

was in our town last week. I met ....

at ....

....

....

....

....

1 Who was the person?
2 When did you meet him/her? Where?
3 Did you ask for his/her autograph? Did he/she write it for you? Where?
4 Why did he/she come to your town?
5 Did you take a photo?
6 How did you feel?

Use your English (Units 11–14)

1 Listen and tick (✔) the correct answer.

1 What did the boy do on Saturday?

a  ☐

b  ☐

c  ☐

2 Where was Fred this morning?

a  ☐

b  ☐

c  ☐

3 Where did the girls meet?

a 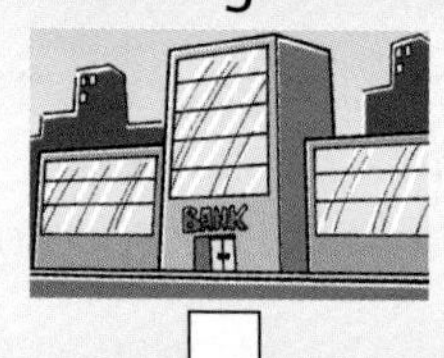

☐

b  ☐

c 

☐

4 How much milk do they need?

a  ☐

b 

☐

c 

☐

5 What did Becky give Ben for his birthday?

a 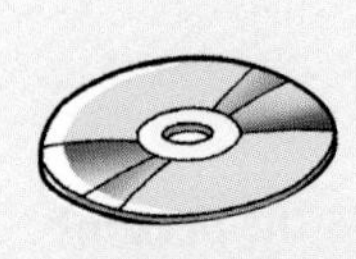 ☐

b  ☐

c  ☐

2 Circle the correct answer.

Rob: [1] How much / How many invitations for the party did you buy?
Katy: Fifty.
Rob: Right. Now, have we got [2] some / any orange juice?
Katy: Yes, it's in the fridge. But we haven't got [3] some / any cola. And we haven't got [4] any / no cheese for the sandwiches.
Rob: That's OK. I can buy some. [5] How much / How many cola do we need?
Katy: Five bottles. And five hundred grams of cheese.
Rob: Five hundred grams? [6] How much / How many sandwiches can we make with that?
Katy: [7] A lot! / Not much.
Rob: Good! Now remember, don't tell Kevin [8] anything / something about the party. It's a surprise!

3 Do the crossword.

Down

1 How … lemonade have we got?
2 How … eggs do we need for the cake?
3 Harry … very hungry, so he ate three cheesburgers.
5 … weren't any fast food restaurants in our town twenty years ago.
9 Can you get a carton … milk from the supermarket?

Across

4 Hey! There's … in the fridge! It's empty!
6 We can't make pancakes. We haven't got … flour.
7 I really liked the sandwiches. They … delicious!
8 Hello. I'd like a burger and … fries, please.

4 Write questions to ask your friend about last weekend.

1 be / busy
Were you busy last weekend?
2 go / to the cinema
……………………………………
3 visit / a friend
……………………………………
4 watch / TV
……………………………………
5 listen / to music
……………………………………
6 do / any homework
……………………………………
7 how much money / you / spend
……………………………………
8 how many films / you watch
……………………………………

Now you can …

✔ Talk about quantity:
We haven't got much juice.
There are lots of apples in the fridge.
A: *How much sugar do you need?*
B: *Two kilos.*

✔ Talk about people, things and places without saying exactly who, what or where they are:
There's someone in the kitchen.
I've got something for you.
They went somewhere.

✔ Talk about the past:
I wasn't at home last night.
I went to the cinema with Jason.

5 Complete with the past simple.

Hi Izumi,
I 1 *had* (have) a great weekend! My father 2 ……………… (take) us to the zoo on Saturday morning. Then, in the afternoon, I 3 ……………… (go) to a new fast food restaurant with Sophie and Mark. The food 4 ……………… (not be) very good, but I really 5 ……………… (like) the milkshakes there – I had three!
I 6 ……………… (not go) out on Sunday. I 7 ……………… (stay) at home all day – I 8 ……………… (want) to finish my new painting. In the afternoon, Harry and Beth 9 ……………… (come) to our house and we 10 ……………… (watch) a DVD.
What about you? 11 ……………… (you / have) a good weekend? What 12 ……………… (you / do)?
Email me soon!
Best wishes,
Lucy

15 Articles: *a / an*, *the*, zero article

1 Complete the table.

a/an	There was .... good programme on TV. That's .... good idea! I want to be .... explorer.
the	I want to sail round .... world. Where's .... Sahara Desert? Let's explore .... park!
zero article	I want to climb Mount Everest. I'd like to visit Africa. Let's play football.

2 Read the information.

a/an

We use ***a/an*** with singular countable nouns:

- when we talk about one thing or person but we don't say exactly which one:
  Lucy's reading a book.
  There's a supermarket near my house.
- to talk about someone's job:
  My mother is a teacher.
- to describe people or things:
  Pip is a nice girl. That's a good idea.
- in expressions with numbers:
  I sleep eight hours a night.
  Apples cost €3 a kilo.
  Remember: We don't use ***a/an*** with uncountable nouns (*water, milk*) or plural nouns (*apples, books*).

the

We can use ***the*** with singular, plural and uncountable nouns. We use ***the***:

- when it is clear which person or thing we mean:
  The boy over there is my brother. Where's the sugar?
- when there is only one:
  The Earth is round. Peter is in the garden.
- with the names of oceans (*the Pacific Ocean*), seas (*the Red Sea*), rivers (*the Nile*), mountain ranges (*the Andes*) and deserts (*the Sahara Desert*).
- with the names of some countries: *the USA (United States of America), the UK (United Kingdom), the Netherlands*
- with musical instruments:
  He plays the piano.
- in some time expressions:
  in the morning/afternoon/evening, at the weekend.
  But we say:
  in January, at night, on Mondays

Zero article

We don't use ***a*** or ***the***:

- with names of people (*Peter, Mr Hardy*), continents (*Africa*), most countries (*Spain*), cities (*Madrid*), streets (*West Street*), lakes (*Lake Michigan*) and mountains (*Mount Everest*).
- with sports (*basketball*), games (*chess*), school subjects (*Maths*), meals (*dinner*) and languages (*English*).
- in these expressions:
  Beth is at home/at school/in bed.
  I go to school every day. I go by bus.

Look!

When we talk about something for the first time, we use ***a/an***. When we talk about it again, we use ***the***: *This is a sandwich and that's an apple. The sandwich is for you and the apple is for me.*

3 Complete with *a*, *an* or *the*.

1 A: This is a boring film. B: Yes, it is. Come on, let's play ..*a*.. game.
2 A: What does your father do? B: He works in .... office.
3 A: What's that? B: It's .... old photo of my dad.
4 A: Joe's mum is .... actress. B: Really? What about his father?
5 A: I can't open .... door. B: Where's .... key?
6 A: Where's Mike? B: He's at .... sports centre with Fred.
7 A: How much are the oranges? B: They're €2 .... kilo, I think.

4 Complete with *the* or – . Then do the quiz.

TeenLink

Geography quiz

Are these statements true or false?

1	.....–..... *New York is in* ...the... *USA.*	*True / False*
2	.... *Paris is the capital of* .... *Spain.*	*True / False*
3	.... *Nile is in* .... *Africa.*	*True / False*
4	.... *Atlantic Ocean is in* .... *Asia.*	*True / False*
5	.... *Alps are in* .... *Europe.*	*True / False*
6	.... *Sydney is in* .... *Australia.*	*True / False*
7	.... *Mount Fuji is in* .... *Turkey.*	*True / False.*
8	.... *Sahara desert is in* .... *UK.*	*True / False*
9	.... *Tokyo is in* .... *Japan.*	*True / False*
10	.... *Lake Superior is in* .... *Netherlands.*	*True / False*

Answers: 1 True 2 False 3 True 4 False 5 True 6 True 7 False 8 False 9 True 10 False

5 Complete with *a, the* or – .

1 A: There's [1] ...a... postcard for you on the table. I think it's from [2] .... Mike.
B: Yes, it is. Oh, look – it's from [3] .... Miami!

2 A: What does this word mean?
B: I don't know. Why don't you ask [4] .... Claire? She speaks [5] .... Spanish.
A: I can't. She isn't at [6] .... home – she's at [7] .... sports centre. She's playing [8] .... tennis with Sarah.

3 A: Do you always do your homework in [9] .... evening?
B: Well, no. But today I'm studing for my Geography test.
A: Oh. I hate [10] .... Geography!
B: I like it.
A: Of course you do! Your mum's [11] .... Geography teacher!
B: Well, yes. But she never helps me with my homework!

6 Complete with *a/an* or *the.*

1 There was .... good film on TV last night. .... film was about Africa.
2 Peter and Lucy live in .... small town. .... town isn't near the sea.
3 Vicky has got .... cat and two dogs. .... dogs are very friendly. .... cat isn't friendly.
4 There's .... sports centre and .... swimming pool in our town. .... swimming pool is in .... park near my house.
5 My mum's got .... old car. .... car is blue.
6 I met .... interesting girl yesterday. .... girl was from Poland.

7 Write true answers to the questions.

1 What are your favourite subjects at school?
My favourite subjects are ....

2 Which country would you like to visit? Where is it?
I'd like to visit .... It's in ....

3 Which is your favourite sport? Who is your favourite player?
My favourite sport is .... and my favourite player is ....

4 What's your favourite food?
My favourite food is ....

5 What do you want to be when you grow up?
I want to be ....

6 Can you or your friend speak a foreign language?
I .... My friend ....

Writing practice

8 Write *a/an, the* or -.

TeenLink

***TeenLink* friends abroad**

Hi!

My name's [1] .... Paul. I'm twelve years old and I come from [2] ....USA. I live in [3] .... big city with my parents and my sister, Tania. [4] .... name of my city is Seattle. My dad works in [5] .... bank and my mum is [6] .... teacher. She teaches [7] .... Spanish in a language school. [8] .... school is in [9] .... centre of Seattle.

My sister and I like [10] .... music very much. I play [11] .... guitar and she sings. We write [12] .... songs together. She writes [13] .... lyrics and I write [14] .... music. I'd like to be [15] .... musician when I grow up.*

**lyrics = the words of a song*

9 Write.

Write to *TeenLink* about you and your family. Use Exercise 8 as a model.

Photo

Hi!

My name's .... I'm .... and I come from .... I live ....

with ....

....

....

16 Comparatives and superlatives

Short adjectives

1 **Complete the tables.**

Adjective	Comparative	Superlative
fast	faster (than)	the fastest
big	bigg......... (than)	the bigg.........
heavy	heavier (.............)	.... heaviest
lazy	lazi......... (.............)	.... lazi.........

2 Read the information.

Use

- We use the **comparative** form of adjectives to compare two people or things:
  I'm taller than Emma.
- We use the **superlative** form of adjectives to compare three or more people or things:
  Tim is the tallest boy in our class.

Form

- To form the comparative of short adjectives, we add *-er* (*than*):
  fast ➜ *faster (than)*
  clever ➜ *cleverer (than)*
- To form the superlative of short adjectives, we use *the* + *-est*:
  fast ➜ *the fastest*
  clever ➜ *the cleverest*

▶ Look at the spelling rules on page 141.

3 Complete the table.

Adjective	Comparative	Superlative
strong	stronger	....
thin	....	....
ugly	....	....
small	....	....
big	....	....
fast	....	....
pretty	....	....
nice	....	....
fat	....	....

Look!

Adjectives ending in -e:
nice ➜ *nicer*
Adjectives ending in vowel + consonant:
big ➜ *bigger*
Adjectives ending in consonant + -y:
heavy ➜ *heavier*

4 Complete with the comparative. Then do the quiz.

TeenLink

General knowledge quiz

Are these statements true or false?

1 Neptune is smaller than Jupiter. (small) True / False

2 Hot water is .... cold water. (heavy) True / False
3 The Mississippi River is .... the Nile River. (long) True / False
4 Mount Kilimanjaro is .... Mount Everest. (high) True / False
5 New York City is .... Los Angeles. (big) True / False
6 Some human bones are .... steel. (strong) True / False
7 Gold is .... silver. (cheap) True / False
8 Europe is .... Asia. (large) True / False

Answers: 1 True 2 False 3 True 4 False 5 True 6 True 7 False 8 False

5 Complete with the superlative.

TeenLink

1 The smallest .... bird in the world is only 5.5 cm long. (small)
2 The blue whale is .... animal in the world. (large)
3 It is also .... animal in the world. (loud)
4 .... fish in the world is the Indo-Pacific sailfish. (fast)
5 The seahorse is .... fish. (slow)
6 .... spider in the world can eat birds! (big)
7 Howler monkeys are .... land animals. (noisy)
8 .... snake in the world was a python. It was almost ten metres long. (long)

6 Look at the table and write sentences.

	Age	Height	Weight
Peter	12	1.66 m	60 kg
Lucy	10	1.52 m	40 kg
Harry	12	1.70 m	65 kg
Beth	11	1.62 m	50 kg

1 Peter / Lucy (old) Peter's older than Lucy.
2 Peter / Harry (short) ....
3 Harry / Peter (heavy) ....
4 Beth / Harry (young) ....
5 Lucy / Beth (thin) ....
6 Beth / Lucy (tall) ....
7 (old) Peter and Harry are the oldest.
8 (short) ....
9 (heavy) ....
10 (young) ....
11 (thin) ....
12 (tall) ....

7 Complete the questions. Then write true answers.

1 Who is the tallest .... pupil in your class? (tall) – is the tallest.
2 Are you .... your teacher? (young) ....
3 Is Chinese .... English? (easy) ....
4 Who is .... person in your family? (old) ....
5 Is your room .... than your mum and dad's? (big) ....
6 Which is .... room in your house? (nice) ....

Long adjectives, irregular adjectives

8 **Complete the tables.**

Long adjectives		
Adjective	**Comparative**	**Superlative**
beautiful	more beautiful (than)	the most beautiful
expensive	.... expensive (than)	the .... expensive
dangerous	more dangerous (............)	.... most dangerous

Irregular adjectives		
Adjective	**Comparative**	**Superlative**
good	better (............)	.... best
bad	worse (............)	.... worst

9 Read the information.

Form

- To form the comparative of long adjectives, we use *more* + adjective (+ *than*):
  beautiful ➜ *more beautiful (than)*
  expensive ➜ *more expensive (than)*
- To form the superlative of long adjectives, we use *the most* + adjective:
  beautiful ➜ *the most beautiful*
  expensive ➜ *the most expensive*
- These adjectives are irregular:
  good ➜ *better* ➜ *the best*
  bad ➜ *worse* ➜ *the worst*

10 Complete the table.

Adjective	Comparative	Superlative
beautiful	*more beautiful*	....
expensive	....	....
interesting	....	....
exciting	....	....
wonderful	....	....

11 Compare the pets.

	●	● ●	● ● ●
1 dangerous	a dog	a snake	a tarantula
2 intelligent	a goldfish	a shark	a dolphin
3 popular	a hamster	a dog	a cat
4 beautiful	an iguana	a goldfish	a parrot
5 expensive	a hamster	a cat	a horse
6 good guard dogs	a poodle	a collie	an alsatian

1 Snakes *are more dangerous than* dogs. Tarantulas .... of all.
2 Sharks .... goldfish. Dolphins .... of all.
3 Dogs .... hamsters. Cats .... of all.
4 Goldfish are .... iguanas. Parrots are .... of all.
5 Cats .... hamsters. Horses .... of all.
6 Collies .... poodles. Alsatians .... of all.

Writing practice

12 **Complete with the correct form of the comparative or the superlative.**

TeenLink

Pet Corner
Here are two letters from Pet Lovers. We're waiting for yours, too!

Hi!
My name's Debbie and I've got a goldfish. Its name's Goldie. It's 1......................... (quiet) pet in the world! Actually, I wanted a piranha fish but they are 2......................... (dangerous) than goldfish. They bite! Also, Goldie is 3......................... (small) than a cat or a dog and my mum likes that because we have a small house, too. A goldfish is 4......................... (clean) than a hamster, so I can keep it in my room!
I love Goldie!
Debbie Lowe (7)

Hello *TeenLink*!
I'm Ruth and I'm eleven years old. I've got two pets! A parrot and a dog. My parrot, Cookie, is 5......................... (noisy) bird in the neighborhood! He sings all day! He's 6......................... (intelligent) than a canary but he's 7......................... (ugly), too!
My dog, Missy, is 8......................... (good) dog in the world. She's also 9......................... (dirty) dog in the world! She hates having a bath!
I think she's 10......................... (beautiful) dog in the world!

13 **Write.**

Write a letter to *TeenLink*. Write about the pet you have or the pet you would like to have. Use the letters in Exercise 12 as a model.

Photo

Hi!
My name's .... and I'm ....
.... years old. ....
....
....
....
....

Adverbs of manner

1 **Complete the table.**

Regular		Irregular	
Adjective	**Adverb**	**Adjective**	**Adverb**
tight	tightly	good	well
careful	carefully	fast	fast
loud	....	hard	hard
quiet	....		
happy	happily		
easy	....		

2 Read the information.

Use

- **Adjectives** describe a thing or person:
  She's a good singer. *He's a slow worker.*
- **Adverbs of manner** describe an action. They tell us how someone does something:
  She sings well. *He works slowly.*

Form and spelling

- To form adverbs of manner, we add *-ly* to an adjective:
  slow ➜ *slowly* *quick* ➜ *quickly*
  loud ➜ *loudly* *polite* ➜ *politely*
- For adjectives that end in *-y*, we change *-y* to *-i* and then add *-ly*:
  happy ➜ *happily*
  noisy ➜ *noisily*
- These adverbs are irregular. We do not form them with *-ly*:
  good ➜ *well* *fast* ➜ *fast* *hard* ➜ *hard*
- Adverbs of manner come after the verb:
  Mrs Smith walks slowly. *Peter runs fast.*
- *fast* and *hard* can be adjectives or adjectives.
  Brian runs fast. Brian is a fast runner.

3 Complete with adverbs.

1 Aunt Agatha is a careful driver. She drives carefully.
2 Harry is a bad player. He plays ....
3 Mrs Hardy is a good cook. She cooks ....
4 Peter's a fast swimmer. He swims ....
5 Mr Hardy's a hard worker. He works ....
6 Lucy is a slow writer. She writes ....
7 Mr Davis is a quiet speaker. He speaks ....
8 Beth is a neat writer. She writes ....

4 Put the words in the correct column.

~~dangerous~~ fast funnily happy hard lazy nice perfectly safely well

Adjective	Adverb	Adjective or adverb
dangerous	....	....
....	....	....
....	....	
....	....	

5 Choose and complete.

1 (careful, carefully)
  a This is very important. Read it carefully.
  b You can use my camera, but be very careful with it.
2 (easy, easily)
  a Of course I can do this exercise! It's very ....
  b Kelly makes friends ....
3 (quiet, quietly)
  a Please be .... Sarah's doing her homework.
  b 'The baby's asleep,' my mum said ....
4 (beautiful, beautifully)
  a She sings ....
  b Those flowers are ....
5 (safe, safely)
  a Don't walk on that bridge. It isn't ....
  b Bye, Dad! Drive ....

6 Choose and complete.

badly carefully clumsy fast hard quick well

Hi Izumi,
The school play is tomorrow, but the scenery isn't ready. Actually, it was ready, but my silly brother fell on the scenery yesterday and destroyed it! He is so [1]................! It's not fair! We worked really [2]................ in my Art class to make it and now we must start again! Luckily, Peter wasn't hurt [3]................ . He's only got a scratch on his knee.

The team from my Art class is great! We can all draw really [4]................ . We have photographs of the things we want to paint and we draw them [5]................ on big pieces of paper. Then we add the colours. We must be very [6]................ because the paint dries [7]................ .
Bye for now,
Lucy

7 Write sentences in the present simple. Use an adjective or adverb.

1 Lucy / be / good / at Art — Lucy is good at Art.
2 Peter / sometimes / work / careless ....
3 Harry and Beth / always / work / hard ....
4 English / be / easy ....
5 our teacher / speak / clear ....
6 Beth / be / always / polite ....
7 Liz's mum / always / drive / slow ....
8 Peter's room / be / very untidy ....
9 I / can't / draw / very good ....
10 that story / be / very funny ....

8 **Choose an adverb to complete the sentences so they are true for you.**

badly carefully fast hard loudly neatly quickly quietly slowly well

1 I work .... in class.
2 I write my homework ....
3 Our teacher sometimes speaks very ....
4 My best friend speaks English ....
5 I like to play music ....
6 I sing ....

Writing practice

9 **Read the review in *TeenLink* about the school play. Then choose a word and complete with its adjective or adverb form.**

bad beautiful (x 2) clear clumsy funny good great ~~hard~~

TeenLink

Prince Rupert the Donkey

The play is about a donkey, Rupert. Rupert works 1 *hard*......... all day. He wants to be a man and stop working. One day, a good witch turns him into a prince – he is now Prince Rupert Donkey. He meets the 2................ Princess Julia and falls in love with her. The only problem is that he can't speak 3................ – no one understands him – because, in his mind, he is still a donkey!

Helen Barnes was very 4................ as Princess Julia. She sang 5................ and her acting was excellent. Tom Good was 6................ as Prince Rupert Donkey – he danced 7................ and sang really 8................ – like a real donkey! He was very 9................. The audience laughed all the time!

10 **Write.**

Write a review about this school play for *TeenLink*. Use Exercise 9 as a model. Try to use six adverbs in your review.

Wobble the Wizard

The .... *is about* ....
....
....
The actors were .... *and* ....
....
The acting was ....
....
....

Young girl, Jenny, works hard but very poor.
She meets Wizard Wobble.
Wizard Wobble intelligent and kind but his magic is not very good.
Very funny play.
Sue Brown played Jenny: good singer, very pretty
Joe Smith played Wobble: funny, very loud

18 *be going to*

1 Complete the tables.

Statements				
Positive	I	am (.................)	going to	play.
	We / You / They	are (.................)		
	He / She / It	is (.................)		
Negative	I	am not (.................)		
	We / You / They	.... (aren't)		
	He / She / It	is not (.................)		

Questions			
Am	....	going to	play?
....	we / you /		
....	he / she / it		

Short answers
Yes, I .... No, I 'm not.
Yes, we / you / they are. No, we / you / they ....
Yes, he / she / it .... No, he / she / it isn't.

Wh- questions

What When	am	I	going to	play?
	are	you / we / they		
	is	he / she / it		

2 Read the information.

Use

We use ***be going to***:

- to make a prediction, when something in the present tells us that something is going to happen in the future.
  Look at those clouds. It's going to rain.
- to talk about our plans and intentions for the future.
  He's going to have a party.
  I'm going to study Chemistry.

Time expressions

- We often use these time expressions when we talk about the future:
  today, tomorrow, next Saturday/week/month, this week/month/year, in January/the summer, on Monday/Tuesday
  He's going to buy a bike next month.

3 What's going to happen? Look and complete. Use *be going to* and the verbs in the box.

be drop fall kick not win rain

1 It ....

2 He .... off the ladder.

3 Their team ....

4 School starts at 8.30. She .... late.

5 She .... the cake.

6 He .... the ball.

4 **Lucy and Sophie are getting ready for a school trip. Complete Lucy's note to Sophie. Use *be going to*.**

Sophie,
I [1] 'm going to bring (bring) my MP3 player. We don't need any CDs.
I [2] .... (make) some hot cocoa for the journey. And my mum [3] .... (make) some cheese sandwiches for us.
I [4] .... (not bring) my camera. Peter needs it. Can you bring yours?
Ben called last night. He's ill, so he [5] .... (not come) with us.
My father [6] .... (drive) us to school. Let's meet at my house at eight o'clock.

5 **What is Beth going to do next week? Look at her notes and complete the questions with *be going to*. Then answer them.**

Monday	finish report for school paper
Tuesday	study for English test
Wednesday	go to the hairdresser's (6.00 p.m.)
Thursday	buy present for Peter
Friday	meet Harry at sports centre (5.00 p.m.)
Saturday	have lunch with Angela (1.00 p.m.)
Sunday	visit Uncle Bob

Look!
Is she going to visit her uncle on Sunday?
Yes, she is. ✔ ~~*Yes, she's going.*~~

1 Is she going to visit her uncle on Sunday? (visit) Yes, she is.
2 .... her report on Wednesday? (finish) ....
3 .... a present for Peter on Thursday? (buy) ....
4 .... Harry on Friday? (meet) ....
5 .... lunch with Angela on Monday? (have) ....
6 .... for her test on Tuesday? (study) ....
7 .... to the hairdresser's on Saturday? (go) ....

6 **Read and complete with *be going to*.**

1 A: What .... at the weekend? (you / do)
B: I .... to the cinema with Tim. (go)
A: What film .... ? (you / see)
B: We .... the new Bond film. (see)
2 A: My cousin .... us soon. (visit)
B: How long .... ? (she / stay)
A: For a week.
B: What .... with her? (you / do)
A: We .... shopping in London. (go)
3 A: .... anywhere in the school holidays? (you / go)
B: Yes, I .... to Eurodisney with my family. (go)
A: Where .... ? (you / stay)
B: We .... in a hotel. (not stay)
We .... camping. (go)

7 **Write questions with *be going to*. Then write true answers.**

1 what / you / do / at the weekend?
What are you going to do at the weekend? ....

2 you / stay / at home?
....

3 what time / you / get up / on Saturday?
....

4 your best friend / visit / you / on Sunday?
....

5 where / you / go / on holiday?
....

6 you / have / a party on your birthday?
....

Writing practice

8 **Look, read and write.**

Harry's class is preparing for the school fair. Read Harry's notes and complete his email.

Dear Mrs Jackson,
Here's the list of preparations for the School Fair:
Peter and I are going to paint the stalls.
Kevin and Diana ....
Brian and Tina ....
....
....
....
Harry Davis

Spring School Fair – May 6th	
Peter + Harry	paint the stalls
Kevin + Diana	sell second-hand books
Brian + Tina	make paper kites
Tom	bring sound system
Vicky + Brian	play music
Alex	sell drinks and food
The whole class	clean up after the fair

9 **Write.**

Your class is preparing for a school picnic next week. Write a note to your class teacher and say what you and your friends are going to do. Use Exercise 8 as a model.

Dear ....
Here's the list for the school picnic.
I am going to ....
.... is going to ....
.... and .... are going to ....
....
....

19 *will*

1 **Complete the tables.**

Questions			Short answers
Will	I / he / she / it / we / you / they	help?	Yes, I / he / she / it / we / you / they will. No, I / he / she / it / we / you / they ....

Statements			
Positive	I / He / She / It / We / You / They	will ('ll)	help.
Negative	I / He / She / It / We / You / They	will .... (won't)	

Wh- questions			
Where	will	I / he / she / it / we / you / they	be?

2 Read the information.

Use
We use ***will***:
- to say what we think, guess or know will happen in the future. We often use *I think* and *I hope* with *will*.
  I think she'll help you.
  I hope our team will win.
- when we decide to do something, at the moment we decide to do it.
  Oh, that's the phone. I'll answer it.
  I'll wait here.

There will be
- The future form of *there is/there are* is *there will be*.
  There will be lots of shops here in twenty years' time.
  There won't be many people here.
  A: *Will there be a shopping centre, do you think?*
  B: *Yes, there will.*

3 Complete with *will* or *won't*.

1 Lucy will.......... be a famous artist.
2 She .... be a basketball player.
3 She .... have lots of fans.
4 She .... work in an office.
5 Her family .... be proud of her.
6 She .... live in a small flat.
7 She .... marry a handsome man.
8 They .... have three children.

4 Lucy's talking to Sophie. Read and complete. Use *will*, *'ll* or *won't* and the words in brackets.

1 Lucy: Will I be.................. famous? (I / be)
Sophie: Yes, you will. You 'll have.................. (have) lots of fans!

2 Lucy: .... my paintings? (people / like)
Sophie: Yes, ... They .... them. (love)

3 Lucy: .... at me? (my friends / laugh)
Sophie: No, ... They .... your biggest fans. (be)

4 Lucy: .... a poor artist? (I / be)
Sophie: No, ... You ....lots of money. (have)

5 Lucy: ....my paintings? (people / buy)
Sophie: Yes, ... I ....one, too! (I / buy)

5 **Write sentences. Use the words in brackets and the correct form of *will*.**

1 A: I'm leaving.
B: Wait! I'll come with you. .... (I / come / with you)

2 A: Do you want to come to the cinema with us this evening?
B: Sure! .... (I / meet / you at six)

3 A: Did you call Peter last night?
B: Oh, no! I forgot. .... (I / call / him now)

4 A: Why is Anna crying?
B: I don't know. .... (I / ask / her)

5 A: This computer isn't very good. And it's really expensive!
B: You're right. .... (I / not buy / it)

6 A: It's raining.
B: Really? .... (I / get / my umbrella)

6 **Complete. Use *will/'ll* or *won't* and the words in brackets.**

Lucy: I don't want to go to Aunt Agatha's!

Mrs Hardy: Oh, come on, Lucy. It [1]............ (be) OK.

Lucy: No, it [2]............! It [3]............ (be) boring! We [4]............ (have) tea in her garden, and then we [5]............ (spend) the rest of the day in her sitting room! She [6]............ (not let) me watch my favourite cartoon programme – she never lets us watch TV. Oh, and we [7]............ (have) chicken soup for dinner again! I hate chicken soup!

Mrs Hardy: Lucy!

Lucy: Mum, [8]............ (Aunt Agatha / play) the piano for us again? I hate that!

Mrs Hardy: I don't know! Now, are you ready? Your father [9]............ (be) here soon. We must leave at 12.30.

Lucy: Err... Mum, I don't feel very well ... I have a terrible headache ... I think I [10]............ (stay) here.

Mrs Hardy: Lucy!

7 **Complete. Use *will/'ll* or *won't* and the words in brackets.**

TeenLink

I think our quiet little town [1] will be .... (be) very different in twenty years' time. [2]............ (there / be) a lot of cars in the streets and [3]............ (there / be) a lot of noise, too!

[4]............ (there / not be) many trees or parks, but we [5]............ (have) lots of shops and restaurants. More people [6]............(live and work) here, I think. And the children [7]............ (be) happier – because they [8]............ (have) lots of things to do.

It [9]............ (not be) a quiet little town any more, but I'm sure it [10]............ still .... (be) beautiful!

8 Choose and complete.

become do go not start play study (x 2) visit

Beth: I think [1] *I'll study* .... Geography when I finish school. Lucy, what [2] .... you ....?
Peter: That's easy! She [3] .... Art .
Lucy: Yes, I will but I [4] .... right after school.
I [5] .... my cousins in Australia.
Beth: [6] .... you .... to Australia, too, Peter?
Peter: Maybe. My friend Dave and I [7] .... famous basketball players. We [8] .... basketball round the world.
Lucy: I think there's a problem with that, big brother. Dave is a great basketball player. You aren't!

Writing practice

9 Choose the correct answer.

TeenLink FOCUS ON YOU!

This week Fred Barnes from Manchester tells *Teenlink* about his future.
I want to become a writer so I [1] .... Literature. I think I'll study History, too.
My friend, Bob, [2] .... stay in the UK. He'll study in the USA. He [3] .... to become an astronaut and work for NASA!
After college I'll travel for a year. [4] .... other countries and how other people live. This [5] .... me a lot of ideas for my books.
I can wait! [6] .... become famous? I don't know. But I know I [7] .... to be a really great writer, like J.K. Rowling!

1 a) won't study b) 'll study c) 'll go
2 a) won't b) want c) will
3 a) won't b) will c) wants
4 a) I'll see b) I'll go c) I'll be
5 a) will give b) won't give c) not give
6 a) Will b) Will I c) I will
7 a) want b) won't c) will

10 Write.

What will you do after school? Write to *TeenLink*. Use Exercise 9 as a model.

Focus on you!
This week .... **from** ....
tells *Teenlink* about .... **future**.
I want to become ....
so I'll ....
....

Use your English (Units 15–19)

1 Listen and draw lines.

Chris Emma Sara Peter

Tom Michael Ruth James

2 Look at the picture in Exercise 1 and complete the sentences.

1 Michael is .... person in Chris's family.
2 Sara is .... person in Chris's family.
3 Ruth is .... Emma.
4 Emma is .... Chris.
5 James is .... Tom.
6 Peter is wearing .... sunglasses in the photo.

3 Circle the correct word.

1 A: Come on! You're walking very [1] slow / slowly!
B: No, I'm not! You're walking [2] quick / quickly!
A: Let's cross the road [3] careful / carefully.
B: No, let's wait for the green light. The cars are going very [4] fast / fastly. We can't cross the road [5] safe / safely.
A: You're right.

2 A: This is a [6] beautiful / beautifully picture.
B: My Mum painted it when she was my age.
A: Wow! She could paint really [7] good / well!
B: Thanks. Now she likes taking photos. She's very [8] good / well at it, too.

3 A: I can't read the teacher's note on my homework. The handwriting is very [9] bad / badly.
B: It says you must write more [10] clear / clearly. The teacher can't read your handwriting!

4 Read and complete with *a/an*, the *or* -.

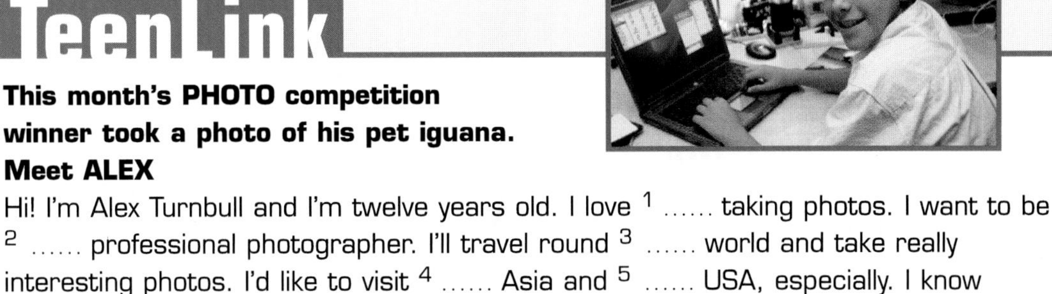

This month's PHOTO competition winner took a photo of his pet iguana.
Meet ALEX

Hi! I'm Alex Turnbull and I'm twelve years old. I love [1] ...... taking photos. I want to be [2] ...... professional photographer. I'll travel round [3] ...... world and take really interesting photos. I'd like to visit [4] ...... Asia and [5] ...... USA, especially. I know languages are important for this job. I can speak [6] ...... Spanish and I'm going to learn [7] ...... Chinese, too!
I like exercise so I usually come to [8] ...... school by bike. I also swim three times [9] ...... week.
I've got two pets: [10] ...... iguana and [11] ...... hamster, Squeaky. [12] ...... iguana's name is Zip. He and Squeaky are best friends!

5 Read and make plans and predictions with *going to.*

1 There are dark clouds in the sky.
It's going to rain.
2 You have an important exam tomorrow.
....
3 There's a great film on TV tonight.
....
4 Your sister wants to be fitter.
....
5 It's your Dad's birthday tomorrow.
....
6 You have some sugar, flour, eggs and butter.
....

6 Complete the dialogues.

1 A: I can't do this exercise. It's very difficult.
B: *I'll help you!* .... (help)
2 A: No-one wants to go to the cinema with me.
B: .... (come)
3 A: Would you like something to eat?
B: .... (have a sandwich)
4 A: This phone looks awful and it's very expensive.
B: .... (not buy)
5 A: It's very cold here.
B: .... (wear my hat)

Now you can ...

✔ Make comparisons:
Andrew is taller than James.
This is the biggest TV in the shop.

✔ Talk about how someone does something:
He runs very fast.
She sang beautifully.

✔ Talk about your plans or make a prediction:
I'm going to do watch TV tonight.
It's going to rain tomorrow.

✔ Talk about your hopes for the future or make a sudden decision:
I'll be a vet when I grow up.
I'll help you clean the house.

20 Present perfect (1)

1 **Complete the tables.**

Statements			
Positive	I / We / You / They	have (.................)	made put packed eaten
	He / She / It	.... ('s)	
Negative	I / We / You / They	.... (haven't)	made .... packed eaten
	He / She / It	has not (.................)	

Questions		
Have	I / we / you / they	made? put? ....? eaten?
Has	he / she / it	

Short answers
Yes, I / we / you / they have. No, I / he / she / it ....
Yes, he / she / it .... No, he / she / it hasn't.

2 Read the information.

Use

- We use the **present perfect** to talk about things we did in the recent past but have a result in the present:

We've put all the bags in the car. (They are in the car now.)

Form

- We use *have* or *has* and the past participle of the verb to form the present perfect. The past participles of regular verbs are the same as the past simple forms. We add -(e)*d* to the infinitive:
  pack ➜ *packed* ➜ *packed*
  play ➜ *played* ➜ *played*
  help ➜ *helped* ➜ *helped*
  live ➜ *lived* ➜ *lived*

- Irregular verbs are different. They don't form the past participle with *-ed:*
  make ➜ *made* ➜ *made*
  buy ➜ *bought* ➜ *bought*
  lose ➜ *lost* ➜ *lost*
  eat ➜ *ate* ➜ *eaten*
  go ➜ *went* ➜ *gone*
  give ➜ *gave* ➜ *given*
  put ➜ *put* ➜ *put*
  read ➜ *read* ➜ *read*
  cut ➜ *cut* ➜ *cut*
  run ➜ *ran* ➜ *run*
  drink ➜ *drank* ➜ *drunk*
  begin ➜ *began* ➜ *begun*

3 Choose and complete the table.

broken brought cut fed found met put read said seen ~~stopped~~ written

	Infinitive	Past simple	Past participle
1	stop	stopped	*stopped*
2	meet	met	....
3	find	found	....
4	feed	fed	....
5	say	said	....
6	bring	brought	....
7	break	broke	....
8	write	wrote	....
9	see	saw	....
10	read	read	....
11	cut	cut	....
12	put	put	....

▶ Look at the irregular verbs list on page 138.

4 Match.

1 I've done my homework.
2 Kate has left.
3 I've locked the door.
4 Peter's broken his leg.
5 I've brought my MP3 player.
6 We've bought some eggs.

a We can make the cake now.
b I can watch TV now.
c Here's the key.
d She isn't here now.
e We can listen to some music.
f He can't play football.

5 Complete with the present perfect.

Are we ready for our holiday?

1 Dad has bought the tickets. (buy)
2 My brother .... a camera from a friend. (borrow)
3 My cousin .... me her MP3 player. (give)
4 And I .... lots of new songs from the Internet! (download)
5 My brother and sister .... goodbye to all their friends. (say)
6 But I .... my friends. I'll phone them tonight. (not phone)
7 I .... my bag. (not pack)
8 And we .... the sandwiches for the journey. (not make)

6 Ask and answer. Use the present perfect.

1 A: Have you done your homework? (you / do)
B: Yes, I have. Can I go to the park now?

2 A: ....? (the rain / stop)
B: No, ... Here, take my umbrella.

3 A: .... the tickets for the concert? (Emma / buy)
B: Yes, ... Here they are.

4 A: .... your brother? (Tim and Alex / meet)
B: Yes, ...

5 A: ....? (Mike / leave)
B: No, ... He's over there.

6 A: .... (you / have) lunch?
B: No, ... And I'm really hungry!

7 Read and write.

Peter, Lucy, Beth and Sophie are getting ready for a picnic.

Beth: So, are we ready?
Lucy: Yes, everything's ready. We're going to have a great picnic! Sophie [1] have you brought (you / bring) the CDs?
Sophie: Here they are!
Beth: Where's Peter? [2] .... (he / buy) the drinks?
Lucy: Yes, he [3] .... He [4] .... (put) them in that bag.
Peter: Hi girls! I [5] .... (bring) Dad's camera. Lucy, [6] .... (you / make) the sandwiches?
Lucy: Yes, I [7] .... They're in the blue rucksack.
Peter: The blue rucksack? But that's Mum's! It's her gym bag. Where is she?
Lucy: She isn't here. She [8] .... (leave)! Oh, no! She [9] .... (take) our sandwiches to the gym!
Peter: Oh great! We've got drinks, music, a camera and no food!

8 Read the information.

just, already, yet

- We often use ***just***, ***already*** and ***yet*** when we talk about recent actions with the present perfect.
- We use ***just*** and ***already*** in positive sentences. They come after *have/has* and before the main verb.
  A: *Where are Mike and David?*
  B: *They've just gone home.*
  A: *Don't forget to tell Anna about the party.*
  B: *I've already told her.*
- We use ***yet*** in negative sentences and questions. *Yet* comes at the end of the sentence or question.
  A: *Does Anna know about the party?*
  B: *No, I haven't told her yet.*
  A: *Have you told Anna about the party yet?*
  B: *Yes, I have.*

9 Complete with *just* and the present perfect.

1 Oh, no! I've just broken my mum's favourite vase. (break)
2 My best friend .... to Manchester. (move)
3 I.................................. the good news. Congratulations! (hear)
4 Look! Your dog .... my sandwich! (eat)
5 I.................................. a very interesting article in *TeenLink*. (read)
6 I.................................. these CDs. Let's listen to them. (buy)
7 Sue .... She can't come with us tomorrow. (phone)
8 I .... the photos from your party. They're great! (see)
9 We .... back from holiday. It was fantastic! (come)
10 Tim and Liz .... a hamster. (buy)

10 Write negative sentences. Use *yet* and the present perfect.

1 A: Can Tina help us? B: I don't know. I haven't asked her yet (I / not ask her)
2 A: Are you hungry? B: Yes, I am. .... (I / not have lunch)
3 A: Is it a good film? B: I don't know. .... (we / not see it)
4 A: Is Ben in the garden? B: Yes. .... (he / not go to bed)
5 A: Are they here? B: No. .... (they / not come back)
6 A: How's Jenny? B: I don't know. .... (I / not phone her)
7 A: Is the homework easy? B: I don't know. .... (I / not start it)
8 A: Are Tom and Pip here? B: Yes. .... (They / not go home)

11 **Peter is very busy today. Look at his TO DO list and write sentences. Use *already* or *yet* and the present perfect.**

TO DO
1 do my homework ✔
2 tidy my room ✗
3 phone Harry ✔
4 feed Cosmo and Bella ✗
5 find my football boots ✗
6 read History book ✔

1 Peter's already done his homework
2 He hasn't tidied his room yet.
3 ....
4 ....
5 ....
6 ....

12 **Look at Lucy's TO DO list. Complete the questions and circle the correct answer.**

TO DO
1 buy a present for Sophie ✔
2 finish Science project ✔
3 send an email to Izumi ✗
4 tell Beth about Sophie's party ✗
5 watch Nature Notes on TV ✔
6 make cake for Dad ✗

1 Has Lucy bought a present for Sophie yet? Yes, she has. / No, she hasn't.
2 .... she .... her Science project ....? Yes, she has. / No, she hasn't.
3 .... an email to Izumi ....? Yes, she has. / No, she hasn't.
4 .... Beth about Sophie's party ....? Yes, she has. / No, she hasn't.
5 ....? Yes, she has. / No, she hasn't.
6 ....? Yes, she has. / No, she hasn't.

13 **Today is Saturday. Complete your TO DO list for today. Choose from these ideas or use your own ideas. Then complete the questions and write answers.**

do my homework wash the dishes
feed the cat/dog/bird clean my room
buy tickets for the concert
download some new songs

1 ✔
2 ✗
3 ✔
4 ✔
5 ✗
6 ✗

1 Have you .... yet? Yes, I have. / No, I haven't.
2 Have you .... yet? ....
3 Have you .... yet? ....
4 Have you .... yet? ....
5 Have you .... yet? ....
6 Have you .... yet? ....

Writing practice

14 Read Harry's postcard to Peter. Complete with one word.

Dear Peter,
I'm having a great time in Paris! I've just come back from the Louvre Museum. It's huge! So far we [1]................ been to two museums. Mum is crazy about them.
I haven't [2]................ the Eiffel Tower yet. We're going to visit it tomorrow, with Louis, my dad's friend. I've just [3]................ his son, Marc - he's really cool. He is a great skater. He [4]................ shown me some new tricks! I'll show you, too, when I come home.
French food is OK. I've [5]................ snails for the first time in my life. They don't taste bad, you know.
Luckily, it's not all museums. I've [6]................ been to the shops and I've [7]................ presents for everyone. But I [8]................ n't taken any photos yet.
What about you? [9]................ you made any plans for your summer holiday [10]................ ?
See you soon,
Harry

Peter Jarvis
25 Oakmead Close
Gramton
W. Yorks
England

15 Read Exercise 14 again. Complete and answer the questions.

1 *Has Harry been* (be) to the Louvre Museum yet? *Yes, he has.*
2 .... (visit) the Eiffel Tower ....? ....
3 .... (be) to the shops ....? ....
4 .... (buy) presents for his friends ....? ....
5 .... (take) any photos ....? ....
6 .... (write) any postcards ....? ....

16 Write.

You are on holiday abroad or in your country. Write a postcard to your friend. Use Harry's postcard in Exercise 14 as a model and the questions below.

Dear
I'm having a great time in ....!
I've just ....
....
....
....

Have you visited any museums?
Have you seen any monuments?
Have you met any new people?
Have you eaten anything unusual?
Have you bought any presents or souvenirs?
Have you taken any photos?

21 Present perfect (2)

1 Complete the table.

Positive	I'................ visited a theme park.
Negative	I've never visited a theme park. I haven't .... a theme park.
Question	Have you ever visited a theme park?

2 Read the information.

- We often use the **present perfect** to talk about something that happened in the past, but we don't say exactly when it happened. We often use it to talk about our experiences, the things we have or have not done in our lives.
  I've visited theme park.
  I've been on a water ride.
- We often use ***ever*** and ***never*** with the present perfect when we talk about our experiences.
- We use ***ever*** in questions.
  Have you ever ridden on a roller coaster?
- We use ***never*** in positive sentences. Be careful: *never* has a negative meaning, but we use it with positive verbs.
  I've never been on a water ride.
  (= *I haven't been on a water ride.*) ✔
  ~~*I haven't never been on a water ride.*~~

3 Look at the table and write sentences in the present perfect. Then complete the table and write about you, too.

	Harry	Beth	Peter and Lucy	....
been camping	✗	✔	✔	....
slept in a tent	✗	✔	✔	....
lit a fire	✗	✗	✔	....
cooked food on a fire	✗	✔	✗	....
swum in a river	✔	✗	✗	....

1 Harry / be / camping — *Harry hasn't been camping.*
2 Beth / light / a fire ....
3 Peter and Lucy / sleep / in a tent ....
4 Harry / swim / in a river ....
5 Beth / cook / food on a fire ....
6 Peter and Lucy / swim / in a river ....
7 I / be / camping ....
8 I / sleep / in a tent ....

4 Look at Exercise 3 and complete the questions. Then write short answers.

1 *Has* Harry *ever swum* in a river? *Yes, he has.*
2 .... Beth .... camping? ....
3 .... Peter and Lucy .... in a tent? ....
4 .... Harry .... a fire? ....
5 .... Beth .... food on a fire? ....
6 .... Peter and Lucy .... in a river? ....
7 .... you .... food on a fire? ....
8 .... you .... in a tent? ....

5 **Write sentences. Use the present perfect with *never*. Then say if the sentences are true or false for you.**

			True / False
1	I / never / be / on TV	*I've never been on TV.*	....
2	my dad / never / try / Mexican food	....	....
3	my best friend / never / play / chess	....	....
4	my brother / never / see / a dolphin	....	....
5	my parents / never / be / to Spain	....	....
6	I / never / climb / a mountain	....	....
7	my friends and I / never / fly / in a helicopter	....	....
8	my grandmother / never / use / a computer	....	....

6 **Write questions. Use the present perfect with *ever*. Then write true answers.**

1 you / ever / visit / Disneyland?
Have you ever visited Disneyland? .... *Yes, I have. / No, I haven't.*

2 you / ever / win / a prize?
....

3 you / ever / be / to another country?
....

4 you / ever / meet / a famous person?
....

5 your parents / ever / take / you to a theme park?
....

6 your mum / ever / ride / a horse?
....

7 your best friend / ever / send / you a postcard from another country?
....

8 you / ever / stay / in a hotel?
....

7 **Complete with the present perfect.**

1 A: [1] *Have you read* .... (you / read) this article?
B: No, I [2] .... What is it about?
A: It's about the Scoop Sisters – that new indie band.
B: The Scoop Sisters? I [3] .... (never / hear) of them.
A: They're great. Here – this is their new CD. Let's listen to it.
B: [4] .... (you / ever / see) them in concert?
A: Yes, I [5] .... They're fantastic.

2 A: [6] .... (you / ever / visit) this website? It's really cool!
B: No, I [7] .... But my brother uses it all the time.
He downloads lots of songs from that website.
A: I [8] .... (never / download) music from the Internet.
B: It's very easy. Here – let me show you.

Writing practice

8 Read, choose and complete with the present perfect.

~~win ✔~~ fly ✔ climb ✗ ride ✔ drive ✗ be ✗
be ✔ ~~swim ✗~~ ride ✗ climb ✔

Kevin's family is very unusual. Read all about them in Kevin's article for *TeenLink*.

TeenLink

The people in my family have done very exciting things in their lives, but they haven't done some simple things, yet. For example:
My dad 1 has won .... an Olympic medal for swimming but he 2 has never swum .... in the sea!
My mum 3 .... Mount Everest, but she 4 .... a tree!
My two uncles 5 .... to the jungle, but they 6 .... to a zoo.
My granny 7 .... a plane, but she 8 .... a car!
Finally, there's me – I 9 .... a camel, an elephant and a llama, but I 10 .... a bike!

9 Write.

Write an article about your family for *TeenLink*. Write about things they have done and things they haven't done yet. Use Exercise 8 and these ideas to help you.

The people in my family have done a lot of things in their lives, but they haven't done other things yet. For example:

My mum has .... *, but she hasn't* .... ,
My dad .... ,
My .... ,
My .... ,
My .... ,
Finally, there's me – .... ,
.... ,

fly in a helicopter
climb the Eiffel Tower
win a prize
do an extreme sport
meet a famous person
be on TV
ride on a roller coaster
see a wild animal
win the lottery
eat Chinese food
go to Australia
visit a theme park

22 Modal verbs (1): *can, could, must, have to*

can, could

1 **Complete the table.**

	Present		Past	
Positive	I / He / She / It / We / You / They	can play the piano.	I / He / She / It / We / You / They	could play the piano.
Negative	I / He / She / It / We / You / They	cannot (..................) play the piano.	I / He / She / It / We / You / They	could not (couldn't) play the piano.
Questions	Can I / he / she / it / we / you / they	play the piano?	Could I / he / she / it / we / you / they	play the piano?
Short answers	Yes, I / he / she / it / we / you / they can. No, I / he / she / it / we / you / they		Yes, I / he / she / it / we / you / they .... No, I / he / she / it / we / you / they couldn't.	

2 Read the information.

can and ***could*** are modal verbs. Modal verbs are different from other verbs:

- We don't add *-s* in the third person singular.
  She can swim. ✔ ~~*She cans swim.*~~
- We use an infinitive without *to* after a modal verb.
  I can play tennis. ✔ ~~*I can to play tennis.*~~
- We don't make questions and negatives with *do/does* or *did*.
  Can you speak English? ✔ ~~*Do you can speak English?*~~

Ability

- We use ***can/can't*** to talk about ability in the present.
  She can speak Italian. I can't see him.
- We use ***could/couldn't*** to talk about ability in the past.
  She could speak Italian when she was three.
  I couldn't sleep last night.

Permission

- We use ***Can I/Can we ...?*** to ask if it is OK to do something.
  Can I use your phone?
  Can we leave now?
- We use ***You can/can't*** to tell someone that it is or isn't OK to do something.
  You can park over there.
  You can't use that computer.
  A: *Can I borrow your camera?*
  B: *Yes, you can. / No, you can't.*

3 Complete with *can/can't.*

1 A: *Can* .... your sister play the guitar?
B: No, she can't.

2 A: I .... lock the door. I've lost the key.
B: Where is it?

3 A: I .... do this exercise.
B: I'll help you!

4 A: .... penguins fly, Mum?
B: No, they ....

5 A: He's only a baby. He .... walk.
B: How old is he?

6 A: She .... sing really well.
B: Yes. She's fantastic!

7 A: .... your father use a computer?
B: Yes, he ....

8 A: I'm sorry. I .... help you.
B: That's OK. I'll ask Jo.

4 Complete with *could/couldn't.*

1 He *couldn't* .... come to the party because he was ill.
2 .... you ride a bike when you were six?
3 Jack was a very clever child. He .... read when he was five.
4 We .... go to the cinema yesterday. We were very busy.
5 Swimming's easy! I .... swim when I was four.
6 .... you speak English five years ago?
7 She speaks five languages. She .... speak Italian and French when she was six.
8 My brother .... play football three years ago, but he's very good at it now.

5 Circle the correct answer.

1 A: My brother [1] can / could play chess when he was six.
B: Really? [2] Can / Could you play chess when you were little?
A: No, I [3] can't / couldn't. But I [4] can / could play now.

2 A: What's the matter?
B: I'm tired. I went to bed early last night but I [5] can't / couldn't sleep because it was really hot! And now I've got a headache and I [6] can't / couldn't do my homework!

3 A: I [7] can't / couldn't find my keys. Have you seen them?
B: No, sorry. Are you leaving?
A: Yes. I'm going to the sports centre with Mark. [8] Can / Could you come?
B: No, I [9] can't / couldn't. I'm busy. I want to finish my Science project. I [10] can't / couldn't finish it last night.

6 Write sentences with *can/can't*.

During the exam:

1 You can use your dictionaries .... (use your dictionaries ✔)
2 .... (open your books ✗)
3 .... (write with a pen or a pencil ✔)
4 .... (take notes ✔)
5 .... (leave the classroom ✗)
6 .... (speak to each other ✗)
7 .... (show your answers to another student ✗)
8 .... (ask your teacher for help ✔)

7 Complete with *can* or *can't*.

1 A: Excuse me, [1] can .... we sit here?
B: I'm sorry, you [2] .... But you [3] .... sit over there.

2 A: [4] .... I use your computer, Mr Green?
B: Yes, of course you [5] .... You [6] .... use the printer, too if you need it.

3 A: [7] .... I listen to your new CD?
B: No, you [8] ....! You broke my favourite CD last week, remember?
A: I'll be very careful. Please?
B: Oh, OK. You [9] .... take it. But you [10] .... use my CD player! You've got one in your room!

must, have to

8 **Complete the tables.**

must	
Positive	You must tidy the living room.
Negative	The cats must .... (mustn't) come into the house.

have to			
Positive	I / We / You / They	have to go out.	
	He / She / It	has .... go out.	
Negative	I / We / You / They	do not / don't	have to .... out.
	He / She / It	does not /	
Question	Do	I / we / you / they	.... to go out?
	....	he / she / it	
Short answers	Yes, I / you / we / they do.		
	No, I / you / we / they		
	Yes, he / she / it		
	No, he / she / it doesn't		

9 Read the information.

must

must is a modal verb. We use an infinitive without *to* after it.

- We use *must* to say that something is necessary.
  *You **must** stay here.*
  We must do our homework.
- We use ***must not/mustn't***:
  to tell someone not to do something:
  Be quiet!
  You mustn't talk in the library.
  to say that it is necessary not to do something:
  We mustn't be late.
- We don't usually use *must* in questions.

have to

- We use an infinitive after ***have to***, but it is not a modal verb. We make questions and negatives with *do/does/don't/doesn't.*
  I have to go.
  He doesn't have to get up early.
  Do we have to leave?
- In positive sentences, *have to/has to* is like *must*. We use it to say that something is necessary.
  We have to stay here.
  He has to do his homework.
- In negative sentences, we use *don't/doesn't have to* to say that something is not necessary.
  We don't have to do this now. We can do it later.

10 Complete with *must* or *mustn't*.

Class rules

1 You mustn't be late.
2 You .... always remember to bring everything you need for the class.
3 You .... listen carefully when your teacher or a classmate is speaking.
4 You .... eat or drink in the classroom.
5 You .... raise your hand to speak.
6 You .... run in the classroom or in the halls.

11 Complete with the correct form of *have to*.

1 I have to get up at 7.30 every day. (get up)
2 We don't have to wait for them. We can go home. (not wait)
3 Tony .... his History project today. (finish)
4 We .... there at eight o'clock. (be)
5 My mum drives us to school. We .... the bus. (not take)
6 We .... at home. We can go to the park. (not stay)
7 I .... my room every week. (clean)
8 It's Sunday. We .... to school. (not go)
9 Gemma .... a dictionary. She can borrow her brother's. (not buy)
10 A: .... this now? (we / do)
B: Yes, ...
11 .... on Saturdays? (your mum / work)
12 A: .... your project today? (you / finish)
B: No, ...

12 Choose and complete the conversation about Aunt Agatha's visit.

can (x 2) can't do don't (x 2) have must

Mum: Now, remember children.
You [1] .... be very quiet. Aunt Agatha hates noise.
Lucy: [2] .... we listen to music in the living room?
Mum: No, you [3] ....
Peter: Do we [4] .... to take her horrible dog for a walk?
Mum: No, you [5] .... Dad will do that.
Beth: [6] .... Peter and Lucy have to stay at home all the time, Mrs Hardy?
Mum: No, Beth, they [7] ....
Beth: They [8] .... come to my house, then!
Lucy: Oh please, Mum!
Mum: Oh, all right...

Writing practice

13 Complete with one or two words.

TeenLink

Our house rules

I think our house rules are OK. My brother and I [1] can............ go to the park or play with our friends after school, but we [2]................ to finish our homework first. I [3]................ stay up late on weekdays, but I [4]................ have to go to bed early on Friday and Saturday.

I don't have [5]................ get up early on Saturday, but I [6]................ to tidy my room. After lunch, my mum [7]................ to do the food shopping and I usually help her. Then I have to [8]................ my homework.

I [9]................ go out with my friends at the weekend, but I have to [10]................ back home early.

Trevor, 13

14 Write about you. Complete with *can, can't, have to* or *don't have to.*

On weekdays ...	At the weekend ...
I .... stay up late.	I .... go to bed early.
I .... bring my friends home.	I .... do my homework.
I .... go to the cinema with my friends.	I .... tidy my room.
I .... tidy my room.	I .... stay out late
I .... do my homework before I watch TV.	I .... drive my mum's/dad's car.

23 Modal verbs (2): advice, offers, suggestions

1 **Complete the tables.**

Advice	
Positive	You should be careful.
Negative	You ....n't spend all your money on CDs.
Question	Should I talk to my father about this?

Offers	
I'll	I................. help you.
Shall I … ?	Shall .... make the sandwiches?

Suggestions	
Let's …	Let's have a break.
Shall we … ?	Shall we make some sandwiches?
Would you like to … ?	Would you .... to have lunch now?

2 Read the information.

Advice
- ***Should*** is a modal verb. We use an infinitive without *to* after it.
- We use ***should/shouldn't*** when we want to give advice.
  You should ask your mother about this.
  You shouldn't watch so much TV.
- We often use ***should*** to ask for advice.
  Should I talk to Tim about this?
  What should we do?

Offers
- When we offer to do things for people, we can use:
  I'll + an infinitive without *to*:
  I'll take your jacket.
  Shall I + an infinitive without *to*:
  Shall I take your jacket?

Suggestions
- When we want to suggest what to do, we can use:
  Let's + an infinitive without *to*:
  Let's listen to some music.
  Shall we + an infinitive without *to*:
  Shall we listen to some music?
  Would you like + an infinitive with *to*:
  Would you like to listen to some music?

3 Complete with *should/shouldn't*.

TeenLink

How to stay healthy

1 You should eat lots of fruit and vegetables.
2 You .... eat a lot of sweets. They're bad for your teeth.
3 You .... drink lots of milk. It's very good for you.
4 You .... go to bed late.
5 You .... eat four or five small meals every day.
6 You .... try to do some sport. Exercise is good for your body.

4 Give advice with *should/shouldn't*.

1 'I want to get better at school.'
You should work harder. (work / harder)

2 'I must get up early tomorrow.'
.... (not stay up / late tonight)

3 'I've got a headache.'
.... (take / some aspirin)

4 'My best friend is angry with me.'
.... (apologise / to her)

5 'I can't do this exercise!'
.... (ask / your teacher to help you)

6 'I want to lose weight.'
.... (not eat / so much sugar)

5 Complete with *Shall I* or *I'll*.

1 A: I'm hungry.
B: Shall I .... make some sandwiches?
2 A: It's hot in here!
B: .... open the window.
3 A: I can't go to the post office.
B: .... post your letter for you?
4 A: This suitcase is very heavy.
B: .... carry it.
5 A: We haven't got any milk.
B: .... get some from the shop?
6 A: I'm thirsty.
B: .... get you a glass of water?
7 A: I can't do this exercise!
B: .... help you.
8 A: How does this printer work?
B: Wait. .... show you.

6 Complete the suggestions with *Let's*, *Shall we* or *Would you like*.

Shall we get the bus?
No, we can walk.

1 Shall we .... get the bus?
2 .... go to the beach.
3 .... to watch a DVD?
4 .... invite Jenny.
5 .... to go to the cinema tonight?
6 .... go to McDonald's?
7 .... stay at home tonight. I'm tired.
8 .... to play a game?

7 Circle the correct answer.

1 A: I'm so tired! And I've got a terrible headache.
B: [1] I'll / Shall I get you some aspirin. You [2] should / shouldn't work so hard, you know.
A: Yes, you're right.
B: Come on. [3] Let's / Shall we listen to some music. You can finish your project later.

2 A: I'm going to the sports centre with Simon. We're going to play tennis. [4] Do / Would you like to come with us?
B: Yes! Great idea. [5] Let's / Shall we call Craig, too?
A: Sure. [6] Let's / Shall we call him now.
B: OK. Oh, no! I haven't got my racket. Sam's got it.
A: Don't worry. [7] I'll / Shall I give you mine.

3 A: What [8] I should / should I tell John?
B: The truth! You [9] should / shouldn't lie to your friends, Sue!
A: OK. I'll talk to him next week. I haven't got his phone number, so I can't call him now.
B: That's OK. I've got it. [10] I'll / Shall I give it to you.

8 **Choose and complete. Make a suggestion, an offer or give advice.**

answer buy have ~~help~~ ride see watch

1 A: This Maths exercise is very difficult. I can't do it!
B: Don't worry. I'll help .... you.
A: Thanks!

2 A: I've got a terrible toothache!
B: Well, I think you .... a dentist.

3 A: It's Nick's birthday tomorrow.
B: .... him a present, then.

4 A: It's nice and warm today.
B: .... we .... our bikes to the lake?
A: Good idea! .... a picnic, too!
B: Yes, that'll be fun.

5 A: I'm really tired this morning.
B: Why?
A: I watched TV until 12.30 last night.
B: That's silly. You .... TV so late on weekdays.

6 A: Mum, your mobile phone's ringing!
B: I can't answer it. I'm in the bathroom!
A: .... I .... it for you?
B: Yes, please.

Writing practice

9 **Choose and write.**

Let's watch a DVD. I'll make some. ~~Would you like to drink something?~~
Shall I go out and buy some? You should sit down, then.
Shall we watch something else?

A: I'm thirsty!
B: 1 Would you like to drink something?
A: Have you got any lemonade?
B: No, I'm afraid I haven't.
2 ....
A: No, I'll have some water.
B: Are you OK?
A: My leg hurts.
B: 3 ....
A: Yes, OK.
B: 4 ....
A: That's a good idea!
B: The DVD is ready.
Here's your water.
A: I'd love some popcorn, too.
B: 5 ....
A: Great!
B: I think I've seen this film before.
A: Really? 6 ....
B: Yes. Let's see what's on TV.

24 Past continuous and past simple

Past continuous

Lucy: I phoned you at nine o'clock yesterday, but you weren't at home. Where were you?

Sophie: I was running in the park with my mum at nine o'clock.

Lucy: What were you doing at eleven o'clock?

Sophie: I was at the sports centre with my sister. We were swimming.

Lucy: I called again at one o'clock.

Sophie: What was I doing at one o'clock? I wasn't swimming … Oh, right! I was playing volleyball.

Lucy: At three o'clock?

Sophie: I was playing tennis with some friends.

Lucy: Were you still playing tennis at five o'clock? Beth and I were waiting for you at the cinema! You didn't come!

Sophie: Oh, I'm sorry! I was sleeping at five o'clock. I was exhausted!

1 **Complete the tables.**

Statements			
Positive	I / He / She / It	was	swimming. sleep..........
	We / You / They	were	
Negative	I / He / She / It	was not (wasn't)	
	We / You / They	were not	

Questions		
....	I / he / she / it	swim.........? sleeping?
Were	you / we / they	

Short answers
Yes, I / he / she / it .... No, I / he / she / it wasn't.
Yes, you / we / they were. No, you / we / they ....

_Wh-_ questions

What	was	I / he / she / it	doing?
	were	you / we / they	

2 **Read the information.**

- We use the **past continuous** to talk about an action that was in progress at a specific time in the past.
  I was playing tennis at six o'clock.
  (I started playing tennis before six o'clock.
  I continued playing tennis after six o'clock.)
  We weren't sleeping at eleven.
  Was your dad working at eight?

▶ Look at the spelling rules on page 140.

3 **What was Sophie's family doing at six o'clock yesterday evening? Complete with the past continuous.**

1 My father *was washing* .... the car. (wash)
2 I .... my homework. (not do)
3 My brother and sister .... about a party. (talk)
4 I .... to them. (not listen)
5 My mum .... dinner. (make)
6 Our dog .... the neighbour's cat! (chase)

4 **Write questions in the past continuous. Then write true answers.**

1 what / you / do / at / lunch time / yesterday?
What were you doing at lunch time yesterday?
I was ....

2 your family / have / dinner / at / eight o'clock / last night?
Was your family having dinner at eight o'clock last night?
Yes, we were. / No, we weren't.

3 you / do / your homework / at / half past six / on Sunday?
....
....

4 who / you / talk / to / before class / today?
....
....

5 what / you / watch / on TV / last night?
....
....

6 it / rain / at nine o'clock / this morning?
....
....

Past continuous and past simple

5 **Complete the tables.**

Past continuous		Past simple
Long action		**Short action**
He .... carrying a bowl They .... going home It .... snowing	*when*	he fell. we saw them. I got up this morning.

Past continuous		Past simple
Long action		**Short action**
While	we were having dinner, we .... watching TV, he .... tidying his room,	Peter tripped over the rug. the phone rang. his friend phoned.

6 Read the information.

- We often use the **past simple** and **past continuous** together, to talk about something that happened while another action was in progress.
- We use the **past continuous** for the long action, the action that was in progress. We use the **past simple** for the shorter action.
  They were going home when we saw them.
  It was snowing when I got up this morning.
- We often use *when* before the shorter action.
  They were going home when we saw them.
  When we saw them, they were going home.

7 Complete with the past simple or past continuous.

1 Mark and Sarah were watching (watch) TV when I left the house this morning.
2 I was looking for my camera when I .... (find) this old photo of mum and dad.
3 What were you doing when the fire .... (start)?
4 We were talking when she .... (come) in.
5 Jack .... (get) ready for school when I called him.
6 She was crying when I .... (see) her.
7 My father .... (sleep) when you phoned.
8 Uncle Bob .... (wait) for us when we arrived at the station.

8 Complete with the past simple or past continuous.

1 When I phoned (phone) Kelly, she was studying (study) for a test.
2 My mother and I .... (clean) the house when Aunt Victoria .... (knock) at the door.
3 It .... (rain) when we .... (go) to bed last night.
4 When we .... (see) Ken and Alex, they .... (play) tennis.
5 When my mother .... (walk) into my room, I .... (listen) to my new CD.
6 When I .... (get up), my parents .... (have) breakfast.
7 Mrs Graham .... (wait) for the bus when she .... (see) the accident.
8 We .... (have) dinner when the phone .... (ring).

9 Read the information.

- We can also use *while* before the past continuous when we talk about something that happened while another action was in progress.
  While we were watching TV, the phone rang.
- Be careful! We use:
  when + past simple:
  When the phone rang, we were watching TV.
  while + past continuous:
  While we were watching TV, the phone rang.

10 Circle the correct answer.

1 I was doing my homework when / while my father came home.
2 When / While we were watching TV, the lights went out.
3 When / While you were sleeping, Dave phoned.
4 Ben was walking home from school when / while he found €10 in the street.
5 I was writing an email to a friend when / while my parents came back.
6 When / While I was talking to Sarah, Tim walked into the room.

11 Complete with the past simple or past continuous.

1 I *was reading* (read) a book when I *heard* (hear) a strange noise.
2 While we .... (swim), it .... (start) to rain.
3 I .... (get) ready for the party when my friend .... (phone) me.
4 We .... (shop) when we .... (see) them.
5 While they .... (drive) down Green Street, the police .... (stop) them.
6 I .... (find) this key while I .... (tidy) my room.
7 My father and I .... (play) chess when my cousins .... (arrive).
8 My mum .... (have) tea with her friend when I .... (arrive).

12 Complete with one word.

1 A: What [1] *were* you doing [2] .... I called you last night? Were [3] .... watching TV?
B: No. I [4] .... trying to finish my homework. And my brother and his friend [5] .... playing the drums! It was awful!

2 A: [6] .... it raining [7] .... you left the house this afternoon?
B: No, but it [8] .... raining when we came out of the cinema. And we [9] ....n't have an umbrella!
A: [10] .... did you do?
B: I called my mum. She came and picked us up.

3 A: I [11] .... playing football yesterday [12] .... I saw a snake in our garden.
B: [13] .... it hiding in the grass?
A: No, it [14] .... It was sleeping under my bike!
B: [15] .... you scream!
A: [16] .... , I did!

Writing practice

13 Choose and complete with the past simple or the past continuous.

carry go ~~play~~ run sit start

Harry was at Peter's house yesterday. The two boys were in Peter's room. They [1] ..were playing.. a computer game when Mrs Hardy, Peter's mum, opened the door. 'Dinner's ready!' she said. When Peter and Harry [2] .... to the kitchen, Lucy was putting the plates on the table. Harry [3] .... down at the table.

Mrs Hardy filled a big bowl with spaghetti and tomato sauce and gave it to Peter. While he [4] .... the bowl to the table, Peter tripped and the bowl flew into the air. Unfortunately, the spaghetti landed on Harry!

Harry went to his house next door and changed clothes, but it wasn't his lucky day! While he was walking back to Peter's house, it [5] .... to rain. He didn't have an umbrella so he ran back to his house. While he [6] ...., he slipped and fell into a pool of muddy water!

14 Choose and complete Peter's story with the past simple or the past continuous.

jump on the table put the sandwiches on a plate laugh eat one of the sandwiches play a computer game wash our hands come into the room get some orange juice

I was at Harry's house yesterday. We [1] .... in his room when his mum came in. 'Would you like a sandwich?' she said. We were very hungry and we said 'yes'. While I was finishing the game, Cosmo, Harry's cat [2] .... and started miaowing. 'I think he's hungry,' Harry said. 'I'll get him some cat food.'

When we went into the kitchen his mum [3] .... They looked delicious! While I [4] .... from the fridge, Harry opened the cupboard and took out a tin of cat food. 'Let's wash our hands first,' I said. 'Yes,' said Harry. He left the tin of cat food on the table and we went to the bathroom. While we [5] .... , we heard a loud noise. We ran to the kitchen. The tin of cat food was rolling on the floor and Cosmo [6] .... ! When we looked at Harry's mum she [7] .... 'While I wasn't looking, Cosmo [8] .... and took one of the sandwiches. Next time I'll ask him if he wants a sandwich, too!' she said.

25 Questions and question tags

Yes / No questions

Peter: How did you get into my house?
Blop: The window was open!
Peter: You aren't going to hurt me, are you?
Blop: No, I'm not.
Peter: What do you want?
Blop: I want the cleverest person in this house. I'm going to take him to planet Zop.

Peter: I'm not clever at all! Take my sister, Lucy! She's cleverer than I am.
Harry: Is he having a dream?
Lucy: Yes, he is. Poor Peter! He's right, isn't he!

1 **Complete the table.**

Yes/No questions	Short answers
Are you ready?	Yes, I am.
1 .... Ben got a bike?	No, he hasn't.
Does Kelly live in London?	Yes, she does.
Are your parents working?	No, they aren't.
2 .... you busy on Sunday?	Yes, I was.
Did he call you last night?	Yes, he did.
3 .... you going to buy that CD?	No, I'm not.
Will they move to France?	Yes, they will.
4 .... they left?	No, they haven't.
Can I use your computer?	Yes, you can.
5 .... you play tennis two years ago?	No, I couldn't.
Should I tell him the truth?	Yes, you should.
6 .... you watching TV at nine o'clock?	No, we weren't.
Have you seen this film?	Yes, I have.

2 Read the information.

Yes/No questions

- ***Yes/No*** questions are questions we can answer with *yes* or *no*.
- Yes/No questions begin with an auxiliary verb (e.g. *be*, *have*, *do/does*, *did*) or a modal verb (e.g. *can*, *could*, *will*).

Do you like pop music?
Was he at home?
Can I use your phone, please?

- We usually use short answers to answer *Yes/No* questions. We use the same auxiliary verb or modal verb in the question and short answer.

A: *Do they live here?* B: *Yes, they do.*
A: *Have you finished?* B: *No, I haven't.*
A: *Will he forgive me?* B: *Yes, he will.*
A: *Can you speak French?* B: *No, I can't.*

3 Complete the questions with one word.

1 A: Is .... there a park near your house? B: No, there isn't.
2 A: .... it going to rain tomorrow? B: Yes, it is.
3 A: .... your dad speak French? B: Yes, he can.
4 A: .... you speak English five years ago? B: No, I couldn't.
5 A: .... you watching TV at eight last night? B: No, I wasn't.
6 A: .... we do our homework every day? B: Yes, we should.
7 A: .... your parents ever been to India? B: No, they haven't.
8 A: .... you study History when you leave school? B: No, I won't.
9 A: .... you got a brother? B: Yes, I have.

4 Complete the questions and short answers.

1 A: Did .... you do your homework last night? B: Yes, I ....
2 A: .... you and your family live in a flat? B: Yes, we ....
3 A: .... your best friend have any pets? B: No, he ....
4 A: .... your parents buy you a bike last birthday? B: No, they ....
5 A: .... you walk to school every day? B: No, I ....
6 A: .... your mum take you to museums at weekends? B: No, she ....

5 Put the words in the correct order and write short answers.

1 you / have / a computer / got?
....

2 you and your family / in London / live / do?
....

3 a camel / you / ridden / ever / have?
....

4 are / play / you / tennis / going to / on Saturday?
....

5 go to work / your dad / yesterday / did?
....

6 it / raining / was / last weekend?
....

Wh- questions

6 Complete the table.

***Wh-* questions**	
[1]................ are you doing?	I'm making a cake.
Who are you?	I'm Jon.
Which bag is yours?	The red one.
[2]................ did they go?	To the cinema.
When did they leave?	On Friday.
[3]................ car is that?	It's my father's.
Why were you late?	Because I missed my bus.
[4]................ old is your brother?	He's eleven.
How much milk do we need?	Two cartons.
How [5]................ CDs has he got?	A lot!
How often do you go to the sports centre?	Every day.

7 Read the information.

***Wh-* questions**

- ***Wh-* questions** begin with:
  a question word (*what*, *where*, etc.) + an auxiliary verb (*be*, *do*, *have*)
  or a modal verb (e.g. *can*, *could*, *should*) + the subject (e.g. *Peter*, *your mother*, *they*).

Question word	Auxiliary/modal verb	Subject	Verb	
What	is	your name?	–	
Where	are	they	going?	
When	can	we	come?	
What time	does	Peter	get up	every day?
How many books	did	your brother	buy?	
How often	has	she	flown	in a plane?

- We use *which* to ask someone about a thing or person, when there are two or more of them. We often use a noun after *which*.

A: *Which bag is yours?*
B: *The red bag.*
A: *Which keys are yours?*
B: *These ones.*

8 Write the question words.

1 A: What........ did he say? B: He didn't say anything.
2 A: ....'s that girl over there? B: Oh, that's Kim's sister, Mary.
3 A: .... sugar do we need for the cake? B: 250 grams.
4 A: .... are you going to stay? B: In a hotel.
5 A: .... did you see her? B: Last night.
6 A: .... eggs do we need? B: Four.
7 A: .... do you have to stay at home? B: Because I have to do my homework.
8 A: .... bike is this? B: It's mine.

9 Complete the questions.

1 A: How much *milk have we got* ? B: We've got three cartons.
2 A: Why .... ? B: I'm crying because I can't go to Jim's party!
3 A: Who .... ? B: It's my brother.
4 A: What .... ? B: I think they're drinking tea.
5 A: Where .... ? B: Cosmo? He's in his basket.
6 A: Whose .... ? B: Which bag? Oh, that one? It's Jenny's.
7 A: How often .... ? B: We usually visit them once a month.
8 A: How much .... ? B: Not much. I've only got £5.

10 Put the words in the correct order. Then match the questions to the answers.

1 does / this camera / how / work?
How does this camera work?
2 I / do / should / what?
....
3 going / were / they / where?
....
4 start / the film / when / did?
....
5 running / is / Tessa / why?
....
6 CDs / buy / did / how many / you?
....
7 bag / that / whose / is?
....

a Ten minutes ago.
b I think it's Fred's.
c You should talk to your father.
d Three.
e Here, let me show you.
f Because she's late.
g Home, I think.

11 Read and complete.

Lucy: 1 *Who's that girl* ? (be / that girl)
Sophie: She's a new student.
Lucy: 2 .... ? (be / her name)
Sophie: Amparo.
Lucy: That's a strange name. 3 .... ? (she / come from)
Sophie: Spain.
Lucy: 4 .... ? (she / speak English)
Sophie: Yes, she can. Her mother's English.
Lucy: 5 .... ? (she / live)
Sophie: In Rose Street. Her house is near my house.
Lucy: 6 .... ? (brothers or sisters / she / have got)
Sophie: She's only got one brother.
Lucy: 7 .... to anyone? (she / never / talk)
Sophie: Because she hasn't got any friends here yet.
Lucy: Let's go talk to her, then! She can be our friend!

12 Complete the table.

Question tags			
Positive sentence ➜ Negative question tag		**Negative sentence ➜ Positive question tag**	
That's Jill's house,	isn't it?	That isn't Jill's house,	is it?
You've got a bike,	haven't [1] ....?	You haven't got a bike,	have you?
They live in England,	don't they?	They don't live in England,	do [2] ....?
Your dad's working,	isn't he?	Your dad isn't working,	is he?
He [3] .... late,	wasn't he?	He wasn't late,	was he?
They liked the film,	didn't [4] ....?	They didn't like the film,	did they?
Adam's going to come,	isn't he?	Adam isn't going to come,	[5] .... he?
She [6] .... help us,	won't she?	She won't help us,	will she?
You've finished,	haven't you?	You haven't finished,	[7] .... you?
He [8] .... swim,	can't he?	He can't swim,	can he?

13 Read the information.

Question tags

- **Question tags** are short questions that we use at the end of sentences. We use them when we want to check if something is true, or when we think that the person we are talking to will agree with us.
  That's Jill's house, isn't it? (I'm not sure. I want to check.)
  He can speak French, can't he? (I think the other person will say *yes*.)
- We form question tags with an auxiliary or modal verb (*do*, *have*, *can*, etc.) and a pronoun (*he*, *she*, etc.).
- We use negative question tags after positive sentences.
  You've got a bike, haven't you?
  He was late, wasn't he?
- We use positive question tags after negative sentences.
  You haven't got a bike, have you?
  He wasn't late, was he?
- The question tag for *I am* is *aren't I?*
  I'm right, aren't I? ✔ ~~*I'm right, am not I?*~~

14 Complete with question tags.

1 A: Your birthday's in March, *isn't it*? B: No, it's in May.
2 A: Bill and Pip went to the party, ...? B: Yes, they did.
3 A: You like pizza, ...? B: I love it!
4 A: She can run very fast, ...? B: Yes, she can.
5 A: They were talking about us, ...? B: I don't know.
6 A: He could read when he was five, ...? B: Yes, he could.
7 A: I'm your best friend, ...? B: Of course you are!
8 A: We've got some juice, ...? B: Yes. It's in the fridge.
9 A: You've bought the tickets, ...? B: Yes, I have.
10 A: I should tell him the truth, ...? B: Yes, you should.

Look!
Your birthday's in March, isn't it? ✔
~~*Your birthday's in March, is it?*~~

15 Complete with question tags.

1 A: You weren't listening to me, were you................? B: Of course I was!
2 A: Bob hasn't invited her to his party, ...? B: I don't know.
3 A: You don't play tennis, ...? B: No, I don't.
4 A: That dog isn't dangerous, ...? B: No. Don't worry.
5 A: Your aunt couldn't drive last year, ...? B: No, she couldn't.
6 A: Her name's Paula, ...? B: No, it's Fiona.
7 A: She didn't call you last night, ...? B: No. She was busy.
8 A: You aren't going to wear that dress, ...? B: Yes, I am! I like it.

16 Complete with question tags.

Lucy: Hello. You're Amparo, aren't you?
Amparo: Yes, that's right.
Lucy: My name's Lucy. You know Sophie, [1].................?
Amparo: Yes, I do. Hi, Sophie. Hi, Lucy.
Lucy: You haven't seen Johnny Depp's new film yet, [2].................?
Amparo: No, I haven't.
Lucy: Great! Sophie, we're going to see it tomorrow, [3].................?
Sophie: Yes, we are. Would you like to come to the cinema with us, Amparo?
Amparo: Yes, thank you.
Sophie: You've got a brother, [4].................?
Amparo: That's right. His name's Pedro.
Lucy: My brother's name is Peter. Pedro is Peter in Spanish!
Amparo: That's funny, [5].................?
Lucy: Yes, it is.

Writing practice

17 Write.

You would like a penfriend. Form questions and write an advertisement for *TeenLink*.

TeenLink

Hi there!
My name is .... and I would like a penfriend. Here are some things I'd like to know about you:
How old are you?
....
....
....
....
....

1 how old?
2 birthday?
3 live?
4 brothers or sisters?
5 free time?
6 favourite film star?
7 how often / go to the cinema?
8 speak a foreign language?
9 favourite sport?
10 plans for the holidays?

Use your English (Units 20–25)

1 Listen and match.

Mark ☐ Anna ☐ Tom ☐ Jenny ☐ Patricia ☐ David ☐

a b c

d e f

2 Look at the pictures in Exercise 1. Choose a verb from the box and complete the sentences.

break buy fly make ~~ride~~ visit

1 *Mark has visited* .... China.
2 .... leg.
3 .... a cake.
4 .... a plane.
5 .... a camel.
6 .... a present for Mum.

3 Read the rules and complete the text with *must/musn't, don't have to, can/can't.*

SCHOOL RULES

Be at school before eight o'clock!
Don't be late!
No jewellery or make-up at school
At breaktime, play in the classroom or in the school yard. Don't go out of the school!

Lessons start at 8.10 so we [1] *must* .... be at school before eight o'clock. We [2] .... be late for class.

We [3] .... wear a uniform. We [4] .... wear our regular clothes, but we [5] .... wear jewellery or make-up.

During the break we [6] .... all go out of the classroom – we [7] .... stay inside. We [8] .... play ball games in the school yard, talk with our friends or have a snack. We [9] .... go out of the school without permission from our teacher.

4 Read the conversation and choose the best answer (A–F).

Susan: I can't find my MP3 player.
Peter: (1) ....
Susan: No, it isn't. I've looked everywhere.
Peter: (2) ....
Susan: Wait! Here it is! It was on that chair. Silly me.
Peter: (3) ....
Susan: Yes, I have.
Peter: (4) ....
Susan: Good idea. I'd like to watch a film.
Peter: (5) ....
Susan: No, wait. I'll come with you.
Peter: (6) ....
Susan: A comedy, I think. Or an action film.
Peter: Good. Me, too. Let's go.

A You haven't finished your homework, yet, have you?
B Shall I go to the DVD rental shop?
C Is it on your desk?
D What would you like to watch?
E Great. Let's watch a DVD, then.
F You should ask Mum. Maybe she's seen it.

5 Complete with the past simple or past continuous form of the verbs in brackets.

Rick: I [1] ...called... you at 4.30 but you couldn't come to the phone.
Diana: Sorry. I [2] .... (dry) my hair. What [3] .... (do) in the morning? [4] .... (go) to the park with Mark and Tom?
Rick: Yes, I did. We [5] .... (play) football when it [6] .... (start) to rain. We got really wet. What about you?
Diana: I was at home. Dad and I [7] .... (wash) the car when the rain [8] .... (begin)!

Now you can ...

✔ Talk about things ability now or in the past:
I couldn't ride a bike when I was four.
I can speak Spanish.

✔ Talk about rules and obligations:
I must tidy my room every week.
I can't stay up later than ten o'clock.

✔ Give advice:
You should eat more fruit.

✔ Make an offer:
I'll help you wash the dishes

✔ Make a suggestion:
Why don't we go to the park?
Let's open this box.
Shall we have lunch now?

✔ Check if something is true or someone agrees with you:
You live in Moon Street, don't you?
The blue bike is great, isn't it?

Irregular Verbs

Infinitive	Past simple	Past participle
be	was/were	been
begin	began	begun
bite	bit	bitten
break	broke	broken
bring	brought	brought
build	built	built
buy	bought	bought
catch	caught	caught
come	came	come
cost	cost	cost
cut	cut	cut
do	did	done
draw	drew	drawn
dream	dreamed/ dreamt	dreamed/ dreamt
drink	drank	drunk
drive	drove	driven
eat	ate	eaten
fall	fell	fallen
feel	felt	felt
find	found	found
fly	flew	flown
forget	forgot	forgotten
get	got	got
give	gave	given
go	went	gone
have	had	had
hear	heard	heard
hold	held	held
keep	kept	kept
know	knew	known
learn	learned/ learnt	learned/ learnt
leave	left	left
lend	lent	lent
let	let	let
lie	lay	lain
lose	lost	lost
make	made	made
mean	meant	meant
meet	met	met

Infinitive	Past simple	Past participle
pay	paid	paid
put	put	put
read	read	read
ride	rode	ridden
ring	rang	rung
run	ran	run
say	said	said
see	saw	seen
sell	sold	sold
send	sent	sent
set	set	set
show	showed	shown
sing	sang	sung
sit	sat	sat
sleep	slept	slept
smell	smelled/ smelt	smelled/ smelt
speak	spoke	spoken
spend	spent	spent
stand	stood	stood
steal	stole	stolen
swim	swam	swum
take	took	taken
teach	taught	taught
tell	told	told
think	thought	thought
throw	threw	thrown
understand	understood	understood
wake	woke	woken
wear	wore	worn
win	won	won
write	wrote	written

Spelling rules

Plural nouns

- To make the plural of most nouns, we add *-s* at the end of the word:
  desk ➜ *two desk**s***
  game ➜ *four game**s***
  computer ➜ *five computer**s***
- To make the plural of nouns that end in *-s*, *-ss*, *-sh*, *-ch* and *-x*, we add *-es* at the end of the word:
  bus ➜ *three bus**es***
  dress ➜ *six dress**es***
  brush ➜ *eight brush**es***
  match ➜ *two match**es***
  fox ➜ *five fox**es***
- To make the plural of nouns that end in *-o*, we add *-es* at the end of the word:
  a tomato ➜ *two tomato**es***
  a potato ➜ *six potato**es***

but

- For these verbs just add *-s*.
  a video ➜ *four video**s***
  a photo ➜ *two photo**s***
  a radio ➜ *three radio**s***
- *To make the plural of nouns that end in consonant + -y, we change -y to -i and add -es:*
  country ➜ *countr**ies***
  baby ➜ *six bab**ies***

but

- To make the plural of nouns that end in vowel + *-y*, we just add *-s*:
  day ➜ *day**s***
  boy ➜ *boy**s***
- To make the plural of nouns that end in *-f* or *-fe*, we change *-f* to *-v* and add *-es*:
  shelf ➜ *shel**ves***
  wolf ➜ *wol**ves***
  knife ➜ *kni**ves***
  life ➜ *li**ves***
- Irregular nouns change in different ways in the plural.
  man ➜ *men*
  child ➜ *children*
- Some irregular nouns don't change in the plural.
  fish ➜ *fish*
  deer ➜ *deer*

Present simple

- To form the third person singular *(he, she, it)* of most verbs in the present simple, we add *-s*:

  walk ➜ *walks* | *read* ➜ *reads*
  sleep ➜ *sleeps*
- We add *-es* to verbs that end in *-o*, *-s*, *-ss*, *-ch*, *-sh* or *-x*:

  go ➜ *goes* | *miss* ➜ *misses*
  watch ➜ *watches* | *brush* ➜ *brushes*
  mix ➜ *mixes*
- For verbs that end in consonant + *-y*, we change *-y* to *-i* and add *-es*:

  study ➜ *studies* | *fly* ➜ *flies*

but

- For verbs that end in vowel + *-y*, we just add *-s*:

  stay ➜ *stays* | *buy* ➜ *buys*

Verb + *-ing*

- To make the *-ing* form of most verbs, we add *-ing* at the end of the verb:

  sleep ➜ *sleeping* | *walk* ➜ *walking*
  stay ➜ *staying*
- For verbs that end in *-e*, we take away the *-e* and add *-ing*.

  dance ➜ *dancing* | *make* ➜ *making*

but

- For verbs that end in *-ee*, we add *-ing*.

  see ➜ *seeing* | *agree* ➜ *agreeing*
- With one-syllable verbs that end in one vowel + consonant, we double the final consonant and add *-ing*.

  swim ➜ *swimming* | *sit* ➜ *sitting*

but

- For one-syllable verbs that end in two vowels + consonant, we just add *-ing*.

  read ➜ *reading* | *wait* ➜ *waiting*
- For two-syllable verbs that end in a vowel and consonant, we double the consonant if the stress is on the second syllable.

  begin ➜ *beginning*

but

- For two-syllable verbs that end in a vowel and consonant, we don't double the consonant if the stress is on the first syllable.

  open ➜ *opening*

Past simple

- We add *-ed* to most regular verbs:
  help → *help**ed***
  walk → *walk**ed***
  listen → *listen**ed***
- For verbs that end in *-e* or *-ee*, we add *-d*:
  dance → *dance**d***
  agree → *agree**d***
- For verbs that end in consonant + *-y*, we change *-y* to *-i* and add *-ed*:
  study → *stud**ied***
  cry → *cr**ied***

but

- For verbs that end in vowel + *-y*, we add *-ed*:
  play → *play**ed***
  stay → *stay**ed***
- For verbs that end in one vowel + consonant, we double the final consonant and add *-ed*.
  stop → *sto**pped***
  clap → *cla**pped***

but

- For verbs that end in two vowels + consonant, we just add *-ed*.
  wait → *wait**ed***
  rain → *rain**ed***

Comparatives and superlatives

- To form the comparative and superlative of most adjectives, we add *-er* or *-est*.
  small → *small**er*** → *(the) small**est***
  fast → *fast**er*** → *(the) fast**est***
- For adjectives that end in *-e*, we add *-r* or *-st*:
  large → *large**r*** → *(the) large**st***
  safe → *safe**r*** → *(the) safe**st***
- For adjectives that end in one vowel + consonant, we double the final consonant and add *-er* or *-est*:
  big → *bi**gger*** → *(the) bi**ggest***
  thin → *thi**nner*** → *(the) thi**nnest***
- For adjectives that end in *-y*, we change *-y* to *-i* and add *-er* or *-est*:
  happy → *happ**ier*** → *(the) happ**iest***
  pretty → *prett**ier*** → *(the) prett**iest***
- For long adjectives, we use *more* + adjective:
  beautiful → ***more*** *beautiful* → *(the)* ***most*** *beautiful*
  interesting → ***more*** *interesting* → *(the)* ***most*** *interesting*

Word list

Unit 1

age (n.)
copy (n.)
cousin (n.)
editor (n.)
favourite (adj.)
magazine (n.)
neighbour (n.)
reporter (n.)
subject (n.)
team (n.)
twin (n.)

Unit 2

afraid (adj.)
awful (adj.)
basket (n.)
beach (n.)
cat food (n.)
cheap (adj.)
dangerous (adj.)
dark (adj.)
deer (n.)
delicious (adj.)
expensive (adj.)
fish fingers (n.)
ginger (adj.)
grape (n.)
Here you are (phr.)
iguana (n.)
knife (n.)
leaf (n.)
meat (n.)
over there (phr.)
parrot (n.)
postcard (n.)
rucksack (n.)
sharp (adj.)
strawberry (n.)
strong (adj.)
sunglasses (n.)
tail (n.)
tidy (adj.)
trainer (n.)
wall (n.)

Unit 3

apple pie (n.)
aunt (n.)
bowl (n.)
capital (n.)
cheeseburger (n.)
club (n.)
exactly (adv.)
fries (n.)
grandparent (n.)
left (n.)
lovely (adj.)
milkshake (n.)
mountain (n.)
note (n.)
racket (n.)
roof (n.)
salad (n.)
short (n.)
skateboarding (n.)
special (adj.)
upstairs (adv.)
wardrobe (n.)

Unit 4

blond (adj.)
Cheers! (interj.)
cold (n.)
comedy (n.)
competition (n.)
email (n.)
floor (n.)
freestyle (n.)
good-looking (adj.)
ground (n.)
Guess what! (phr)
headache (n.)
History (n.)
jacket (n.)
laptop (n.)
mobile phone (n.)
MP3 player (n.)
pencil case (n.)
stuff (n.)

Unit 5

café (n.)
cap (n.)
chimp (n.)
chimpanzee (n.)
cute (adj.)
fairy cake (n.)
hospital (n.)
ill (adj.)
i-pod (n.)
lamp (n.)
lonely (adj.)
look out (phr v.)
pool (n.)
sports centre (n.)
swimming pool (n.)
swing (n.)
toothbrush (n.)
village (n.)

Use your English (Units 1–5)

quiet (adj.)
Well done! (phr)

Unit 6

add (v.)
alone (adj.)
blender (n.)
busy (adj.)
button (n.)
carry (v.)
cocktail (n.)
enjoy (v.)
feed (v.)
grass (n.)
ice (n.)
mean (adj.)
peel (v.)
pour (v.)
pull (v.)
push (v.)
slice (n.)
slice (v.)
tiny (adj.)
tired (adj.)
touch (v.)
wash (v.)

Unit 7

(the) Earth (n.)
bamboo (n.)
bookshop (n.)
Christmas (n.)
classical music (n.)
cornflake (n.)
cry (v.)
drive (v.)
early (adv.)
fix (v.)
flour (n.)
fly (v.)
get up (phr v.)
gram (n.)
horrible (adj.)
lunchtime (n.)
midnight (n.)
nap (n.)
noise (n.)
north (adv.)
once (adv.)
panda (n.)
picnic (n.)
programme (n.)
questionnaire (n.)
shopping (n.)
spring (n.)
study (v.)
tidy (v.)
trip (n.)
visit (v.)
worry (v.)

Unit 8

always (adv.)
burger (n.)
chat (v.)
cook (n.)
excellent (adj.)
fast food (n.)
free (adj.)
healthy (adj.)
important (adj.)
jeans (n.)
lots (of) (n.)
meet (v.)
muffin (n.)
never (adv.)
often (adv.)
pancake (n.)
restaurant (n.)

sometimes (adv.)
stay up (phr v.)
supper (n.)
unfortunately (adv.)
usually (adv.)
weekday (n.)

Unit 9

at the moment (phr.)
barbecue (n.)
begin (v.)
believe (v.)
brush (n.)
brush (v.)
card (n.)
clean (v.)
college (n.)
dentist (n.)
face (n.)
forget (v.)
grandma (n.)
grandpa (n.)
handball (n.)
hard (adv.)
hate (v.)
lemonade (n.)
meal (n.)
move (v.)
need (v.)
nobody (pronoun)
notebook (n.)
paper (n.)
penfriend (n.)
remember (v.)
right now (phr.)
smile (v.)
steak (n.)
still (adj.)
surprise (n.)
wear (v.)

Unit 10

bored (adj.)
bungee jump (v.)
camping (n.)
chess (n.)
crazy (adj.)
cycle (v.)
exercise (n.)
fond (adj.)
footballer (n.)
gorgeous (adj.)
I'd like (phr.)
interested (adj.)
joke (n.)
keen (adj.)
lend (v.)
model plane (n.)
office (n.)
practice (n.)
professional (adj.)
surf (v.)
try on (phr v.)

Use your English (Units 6–10)

bit (n.)
board game (n.)
especially (adv.)
go for a walk (phr.)
granny (n.)
grow (v.)
rose (n.)
sunny (adj.)
weather (n.)
wonderful (adj.)

Unit 11

assistant (n.)
bar (n.)
bottle (n.)
butter (n.)
can (n.)
chips (n.)
cloud (n.)
cupboard (n.)
doughnut (n.)
downstairs (adv.)
empty (adj.)
mistake (n.)
pocket (n.)
pot (n.)
recipe (n.)
takeaway (n.)
yoghurt (n.)

Unit 12

carton (n.)
chicken (n.)
crisp (n.)
diet (n.)
hot dog (n.)
jar (n.)
juice (n.)
loaf (n.)
omelette (n.)
packet (n.)
report (n.)
soup (n.)
tin (n.)
tourist (n.)
vegetable (n.)
Yuck! (interj.)

Unit 13

asleep (adj.)
bakery (n.)
cafeteria (n.)
carriage (n.)
full (adj.)
gym (n.)
hairdresser (n.)
introduce (v.)
library (n.)
phone call (n.)
postman (n.)
present (v.)
pupil (n.)
star (v.)
teashop (n.)
terrible (adj.)
title (n.)
whole (adj.)

Unit 14

amazing (adj.)
autograph (n.)
bake (v.)
chew (v.)
clever (adj.)
climb (v.)
collect (v.)
concert (n.)
famous (adj.)
fan (n.)
feel (v.)
goal (n.)
leisure centre (n.)
local (adj.)
lose (v.)
outside (prep.)
relative (n.)
sadly (adv.)
score (v.)
spaghetti (n.)
swimsuit (n.)
ticket (n.)
travel (v.)
visit (n.)
weigh (v.)

Use your English (Units 11–14)

Best wishes (phr)
invitation (n.)
painting (n.)

Unit 15

actress (n.)
bank (n.)
boring (adj.)
centre (n.)
desert (n.)
dizzy (adj.)
explore (v.)
explorer (n.)
false (adj.)
foreign (adj.)
friendly (adj.)
grow up (phr v.)
lake (n.)
language (n.)
lyrics (n.)
mean (v.)
musician (n.)
ocean (n.)
ride (v.)
sail (v.)
sick (adj.)
statement (n.)
teach (v.)
true (adj.)
Why don't (you)...? (phr)

Unit 16

actually (adv.)
Alsatian (n.)
anyway (adv.)
bite (v.)
bone (n.)
canary (n.)
cheetah (n.)
collie (n.)
dolphin (n.)
domestic (adj.)
exciting (adj.)
fish (n.)
general (adj.)
gold (n.)
goldfish (n.)
guard dog (n.)
hamster (n.)
howler monkey (n.)
human (adj.)
intelligent (adj.)
Jupiter (n.)
knowledge (n.)
land (n.)
loud (adj.)
lynx (n.)
mount (n.)
mph (abbrev.)
natural history (n.)
Neptune (n.)
noisy (adj.)
piranha (n.)
poodle (n.)
popular (adj.)
python (n.)
reach (v.)
seahorse (n.)
silver (n.)
speed (n.)
steel (n.)
tarantula (n.)
whale (n.)

Unit 17

acting (n.)
audience (n.)
bridge (n.)
careless (adj.)
clumsy (adj.)
destroy (v.)
donkey (n.)
dry (v.)
fair (adj.)
fall in love (phr.)
knee (n.)
magic (n.)
mind (n.)
neatly (adv.)
perfectly (adv.)
play (n.)
polite (adj.)
prepare (v.)
prince (n.)
safely (adv.)
scenery (n.)
scratch (n.)
tightly (adv.)
turn into (phr v.)
untidy (adj.)
watch out! (phr v.)
wizard (n.)

Unit 18

clean up (phr v.)
cocoa (n.)
drop (v.)
journey (n.)
kick (v.)
kite (n.)
ladder (n.)
list (n.)
preparation (n.)
relax (v.)
second hand (adj.)
sound system (n.)
stall (n.)
stay in

Unit 19

all right (phr.)
Art (n.)
artist (n.)
astronaut (n.)
become (v.)
carpet (n.)
Geography (n.)
handsome (adj.)
poor (adj.)
proud (adj.)
writer (n.)

Use your English (Units 15–19)

cross (v.)
fit (adj.)
handwriting (n.)
jumper (n.)

Unit 20

congratulations (n.)
cool (adj.)
download (v.)
huge (adj.)
luckily (adv.)
monument (n.)
pack (v.)
plan (n.)
seat (n.)
snail (n.)
souvenir (n.)
taste (v.)
trick (n.)
unusual (adj.)
vase (n.)

Unit 21

extreme sport (n.)
helicopter (n.)
indie (n.)
jungle (n.)
llama (n.)
medal (n.)
prize (n.)
ride (n.)
roller coaster (n.)
tent (n.)
theme park (n.)
wild (adj.)

Unit 22

classmate (n.)
dictionary (n.)
printer (n.)
raise (v.)
rule (n.)
silly (adj.)
strict (adj.)
what's the matter? (phr)

Unit 23

apologise (v.)
aspirin (n.)
have a break (phr.)
invite (v.)
post (v.)
post office (n.)
toothache (n.)

Unit 24

accident (n.)
arrive (v.)
fill (v.)
go out (phr v.)
hide (v.)
knock (v.)
land (v.)
meow (v.)
muddy (adj.)
pick up ((phr v.)
roll (v.)
rug (n.)
sauce (n.)
scream (v.)
slip (v.)
trip (v.)

Unit 25

hurt (v.)
miss (v.)
truth (n.)

Use your English (Units 20–25)

cross (v.)action film (n.)
break time (n.)
inside (adv.)
jewellery (n.)
make-up (n.)
permission (n.)
regular (adj.)
suggestion (n.)
uniform (n.)
yard (n.)